U.S. NAV

Chronicles

For nearly a century and a half since a group
of concerned naval officers gathered to provide
a forum for the exchange of constructive ideas,
the U.S. Naval Institute has been a unique
source of information relevant to the nation's
sea services. Through the open forum provided
by *Proceedings* and *Naval History* magazines,
Naval Institute Press (the book-publishing arm
of the institute), a robust Oral History program,
and more recent immersion in various cyber
activities (including the *Naval Institute Blog*
and *Naval Institute News*), USNI has built a
vast assemblage of intellectual content that has
long supported the Navy, Marine Corps, and
Coast Guard as well as the nation as a whole.

Recognizing the potential value of this
exceptional collection, USNI has embarked
on a number of new platforms to reintroduce
readers to significant portions of this virtual
treasure trove. The U.S. Naval Institute
Chronicles series focuses on the relevance of
history by resurrecting appropriate selections
that are built around various themes, such as
battles, personalities, and service components.
Available in both paper and eBook versions,
these carefully selected volumes help readers
navigate through this intellectual labyrinth by
providing some of the best contributions that
have provided unique perspectives and helped
shape naval thinking over the many decades
since the institute's founding in 1873.

The U.S. Naval Institute on
THE U.S. NAVAL ACADEMY
THE HISTORY

THOMAS J. CUTLER
Series Editor

Naval Institute Press
Annapolis, Maryland

Naval Institute Press
291 Wood Road
Annapolis, MD 21402

Library of Congress Cataloging-in-Publication Data
The U.S. Naval Institute on the U.S. Naval Academy : the history / edited by
Thomas J. Cutler.
    pages cm. — (U.S. Naval Institute chronicles)
    Includes index.
    ISBN 978-1-61251-988-3 (alk. paper) — ISBN 978-1-61251-989-0 (ebook)
1. United States Naval Academy—History. I. Cutler, Thomas J., date– editor
of compilation. II. United States Naval Institute. III. Title: Proceedings of the
United States Naval Institute.
    V415.L1U63 2015
    359.0071'173—dc23
                                                    2015030902

♾ Print editions meet the requirements of ANSI/NISO z39.48–1992
(Permanence of Paper).
Printed in the United States of America.

23 22 21 20 19 18 17 16 15   9 8 7 6 5 4 3 2 1
First printing

CONTENTS

EDITOR'S NOTE

BECAUSE THIS BOOK is an anthology, containing documents from different time periods, the selections included here are subject to varying styles and conventions. Other variables are introduced by the evolving nature of the Naval Institute's publication practices. For those reasons, certain editorial decisions were required in order to avoid introducing confusion or inconsistencies and to expedite the process of assembling these sometimes disparate pieces.

Gender
Most jarring of the differences that readers will encounter are likely those associated with gender. A number of the included selections were written when the armed forces were primarily a male domain and so adhere to purely masculine references. I have chosen to leave the original language intact in these documents for the sake of authenticity and to avoid the complications that can arise when trying to make anachronistic adjustments. So readers are asked to "translate" (converting the ubiquitous "he" to "he or she" and "his" to "her or his" as required) and, while doing so, to celebrate the progress that we have made in these matters in more recent times.

Author "Biographies"

Another problem arises when considering biographical information of the various authors whose works make up this special collection. Some of the selections included in this anthology were originally accompanied by biographical information about their authors. Others were not. Those "biographies" that do exist have been included. They pertain to the time the article was written and may vary in terms of length and depth, some amounting to a single sentence pertaining to the author's current duty station, others consisting of several paragraphs that cover the author's career.

Ranks

I have retained the ranks of the authors *at the time of their publication.* As noted above, some of the authors wrote early in their careers, and the sagacity of their earlier contributions says much about the individuals, about the significance of the Naval Institute's forum, and about the importance of writing to the naval services—something that is sometimes underappreciated.

Other Anomalies

Readers may detect some inconsistencies in editorial style, reflecting staff changes at the Naval Institute, evolving practices in publishing itself, and various other factors not always identifiable. Some of the selections will include citational support, others will not. Authors sometimes coined their own words and occasionally violated traditional style conventions. *Bottom line:* with the exception of the removal of some extraneous materials (such as section numbers from book excerpts) and the conversion to a consistent font and overall design, these articles and excerpts appear as they originally did when first published.

ACKNOWLEDGMENTS

THIS PROJECT would not be possible without the dedication and remarkable industry of Denis Clift, the Naval Institute's vice president for planning and operations and president emeritus of the National Intelligence University. This former naval officer, who served in the administrations of eleven successive U.S. presidents and was once editor in chief of *Proceedings* magazine, bridged the gap between paper and electronics by single-handedly reviewing the massive body of the Naval Institute's intellectual content to find many of the treasures included in this anthology.

A great deal is also owed to Mary Ripley, Janis Jorgensen, Rebecca Smith, Judy Heise, Debbie Smith, Elaine Davy, and Heather Lancaster who devoted many hours and much talent to the digitization project that is at the heart of these anthologies.

Introduction

IT IS NOT SURPRISING that in the many decades since the founding of the U.S. Naval Institute in 1873, there has been a special relationship between that organization and the U.S. Naval Academy, as both USNI and USNA cohabitate along the banks of the Severn River. The Naval Institute was born at the Naval Academy when a group of naval officers gathered to discuss the Navy's problems and to offer solutions, and it has remained there ever since, sanctioned by Congress and embraced by many generations of caring Sailors who see its unique value.

But it is more than a matter of real estate that has led to the natural symbiosis that these two institutions enjoy. As one of the cradles from which officers of the Navy and Marine Corps are nurtured and prepared for the challenges of national leadership, the Naval Academy is rightfully scrutinized, praised, and critiqued by the Naval Institute, whose primary purpose is to make the nation's sea services stronger through the open forum it provides. Over the decades *many* articles have appeared in *Proceedings* and *Naval History* magazines dealing with the U.S. Naval Academy; the Naval Institute Press has published a number of books on it as well. Sometimes these offerings merely enlighten outsiders and remind insiders of the unique character and history of this school where the best of Athens and Sparta are merged. At other times these writings offer helm orders to keep this vital ship on the proper course, and occasionally there are existential challenges that any worthwhile endeavor must be prepared to endure and ultimately reap the benefits that such exercises can bring about.

A companion volume, *The U.S. Naval Academy: The Challenges*, delves into the various issues that have confronted the Academy over the decades, but this edition of Chronicles presents a number of selections from that large catalog of Naval Institute offerings dealing with the *history* of the Naval Academy. In these pages readers will find articles and excerpts from the Naval Institute's vast archive that record the Academy's founding and chronicle its development over more than a century and a half. It is a rich history that not only illuminates the creation and evolution of a unique national treasure but also reflects the evolving customs and values of the nation that this institution serves in such an unusual way.

1 "The Establishment of the Naval School at Annapolis"

Henry Francis Sturdy

U.S. Naval Institute *Proceedings*
(April 1946): 1–17

THERE HAD BEEN much opposition in the Navy to any attempt to educate midshipmen ashore. It was felt that only by practical experience aboard ship could the youngster, fresh from home, be properly trained for his work as an officer afloat. Though several suggestions for an organized naval school had been made since the permanent establishment of the Navy in 1794, nothing had been accomplished and the only educational facilities available for the midshipmen up to the War of 1812 had been the instruction of the chaplains who had no special qualifications for such work, except a supposedly liberal education. During the War of 1812 provision had been made for a school-master on each of the 74's, which were not completed till after the war, but the small pay, cramped quarters, sometimes shared with their pupils, and a very inferior position aboard ship did not draw men of ability. With the increase of pay to $1,200, in 1835, for duty at sea or at a navy yard, some eminent men began to be drawn into the Service as professors of mathematics. They still, up to September, 1842, had to mess with their pupils, however, and continued to suffer constant interruption of their school work aboard ship.

Beginning with the twenties three unorganized governmental schools had come into existence at the navy yards at Norfolk, New York, and

Boston, for those midshipmen on waiting orders between cruises. The instruction was very irregular, the midshipmen attending or not as they pleased, and discipline, apparently, did not exist. Such lack of education and restraint helped to give rise among the young officers to both intemperance and financial irresponsibility. The early age at which some of the midshipmen entered the Navy, Farragut entering it when only nine, made them peculiarly susceptible to such adverse conditions. Some private nautical schools had come into existence at an earlier date and some of the younger officers had even attended college, one midshipman, indeed, going to West Point. A fourth school established by the government in 1839, at the Naval Asylum in Philadelphia, was really the forerunner of the Naval Academy, for it was on account of their proficiency of attainments at the Naval Asylum School that Professors Chauvenet and Lockwood, Lieutenant Ward, and Passed Midshipman Marcy were selected to be members of the faculty at the permanent naval school to be organized at Fort Severn, Annapolis, by Secretary Bancroft.

But it is doubtful whether even as astute and clever a man as Bancroft could have achieved the permanent establishment of an organized naval school, if conditions in the Navy had not become so bad. During and immediately after the War of 1812, the Navy had been looked up to and esteemed by the people of the United States. Its work had been the one bright spot in the war. Its officers and men had been toasted and feted. By 1840 it had become the object of censure and reproach. The newspapers contained numerous accounts of alleged misdeeds of officers in command. Dishonesty, low morals, and brutality were charged against them. This state of things, Park Benjamin declares, in his history of the Naval Academy, was the result of "the lowered morale of the whole service incident to the severe discipline of the 'smart ships' and the educational neglect of the young officers." The culminating episode was the hanging at the yardarm on the brig *Somers*, in 1842, of Midshipman Philip Spencer, an apparent social delinquent, but with great political influence, his uncle being the Secretary of War, John C. Spencer. Midshipman Spencer was convicted of leadership in a conspiracy to mutiny against the officers and the ship. Though this affair gave basis for another attack against the Navy, it clearly disclosed to the public the existing evils in the method of appointing and educating the midshipmen. As Benjamin so aptly says:

> It showed the absurdity of taking in youths at the behest of politicians without a proper proof of fitness, and the wretched folly of sending bad boys into the Navy as a reformatory, or even subjecting good ones to the wholly unfamiliar influences of naval life afloat without previous preparation.

Rear Admiral S. F. Franklin, in his *Memories of a Rear Admiral*, gives a vivid picture of some of the conditions when he entered the Service in 1841. He had been sent first in the spring to the receiving ship *North Carolina* in New York:

> Finally in September, I was ordered to the Frigate *United States* ... Our trials came on with the night, for, as I have said, our mess-room, which was our bedroom also, was about large enough fairly to accommodate two people, yet twelve of us were huddled together in this apartment like so many pigs in a pen. Our hammocks, instead of hanging loose to the sport of the wind, formed a sort of continuous sheet of canvas, dotted over with mattresses. We could neither turn in or out of them without disturbing our neighbors, causing growling and quarreling which often led to serious consequences. I think there was but one basin for the morning toilet—at the most, two—but we made the best of our inconveniences, and accepted the situation with good grace. Ranged around this luxurious apartment were the lockers for our clothes. They were not ample, but we accommodated ourselves to their capacity, and managed to get on with small wardrobes. . . . There was something very cruel, as I look back

at it, in permitting a lot of boys to be huddled together, with no one to look out for their well-being, most of them only sixteen or under, with no experience, and expected to manage a mess. . . . There was something very faulty in this regard in those days, and we were sufferers, from a bad system. . . . The whole system of Naval education in those days was rough and crude.

Different secretaries of the Navy had urged the establishment of a permanently organized naval school. President John Quincy Adams, in 1825, in his first annual message, stated to Congress:

The want of a naval school of instruction corresponding with the Military Academy at West Point, for the formation of scientific and accomplished officers, is felt with daily increasing at aggravation.

The next year a bill to establish a naval school was introduced in Congress. The Maryland Assembly, sensing "the superior advantages which the city of Annapolis and its neighborhood possesses as a situation for a naval academy," requested that Maryland members of Congress "use their best exertions in favor of the establishment of such an institution."

In the Navy itself there had been successive pleas for some organized plan of education for the young officer. In 1836 a memorial from some 30 midshipmen and about 25 other commissioned officers prayed Congress to establish such a school. Articles criticizing the lack of proper schooling appeared in the *Madisonian* and in the *Army and Navy Chronicle*. Lieutenant Maury, the famous scientist, in articles published in the *Southern Literary Messenger*, aroused the thinking public by his denunciation of conditions, which he thought could be corrected by the establishment of cruising school ships. After the lamentable happening on the

Somers, the officers of the *Vincennes*, in 1844, urged the abolition of "sea professors" and the organization of naval schools; and Commodore Charles Stewart, who had been president of the court of inquiry investigating the hanging of young Spencer, felt that one national school should be established to instruct the midshipmen in international law, languages, mathematics, and the fundamentals of the steam engine. And, indeed, it was this last subject, the study of the steam engine, which aided the advocates for a naval school ashore in winning their fight. In 1839 the first appropriation for building steam warships had been made. So no longer could it be possible to train afloat the midshipmen in all the methods of ship propulsion, and more and more would it become necessary to acquire ashore the necessary knowledge of ship propulsion.

Thus the time seemed ripe for Bancroft to carry to a successful issue his ideas for a single permanent national naval school. Before he had been in office two months, he had asked for suggestions, from four professors there, to improve the Naval Asylum School. And by June 6 he had come to the conclusion that Annapolis would be a more suitable place. He had to achieve, however, the seemingly impossible task not only of gaining approval of the Navy itself for such a school, but also of establishing it without recourse to additional appropriations, to avoid the danger of Congressional opposition. Part of this task he successfully accomplished through the co-operation of the Secretary of War, William L. Marcy, who was undoubtedly influenced by his son, Passed Midshipman Samuel Marcy, an assistant in navigation to Professor Chauvenet at the Naval Asylum School. Secretary Marcy, in August, 1845, with the approval of President Polk, had transferred to the Navy, for use as a naval school, Fort Severn, which had been built in Annapolis, in 1808, as a defense against an invading enemy penetrating the waters of the Chesapeake. This site had been approved in June, 1845, by the Naval Asylum School Examining Board, apparently through the influence of Commodore Isaac Mayo, who owned a farm about 8 miles from Annapolis and who, in the words of Professor Lockwood, as quoted by Benjamin, "believed that the world revolved around that place" (Annapolis). Thus Secretary Bancroft gained the approval of the high-ranking older officers to organize a permanent naval school. He had presented the problem to them in such a way that it became a question of not whether a school should be organized but where it should be located. A second board of younger officers, Commanders McKean, Buchanan, and Dupont was appointed by Secretary Bancroft, shortly after, to consider again the subject. It also approved of Annapolis and recommended Chauvenet, Lockwood, Ward, and Marcy to be transferred from the Naval Asylum School to Annapolis. Bancroft had now gained the approval of the Navy for his revolutionary change in American naval education.

Though he had surmounted a part of the financial difficulty of his task by acquiring from the Army, without cost, the site and buildings at Fort Severn, he still had to find the necessary means to maintain the school without recourse to Congress. Fortunately for him the $28,200 used annually for the pay of the naval professors and the teachers of languages was designated merely for "instruction." Bancroft, therefore, during the year 1845–46 by gradually placing on waiting orders, without pay, half of the instructors, most of whom were attached to various ships, obtained, without recourse to Congress, the necessary funds for establishing the naval school at Annapolis. The obstacles had been surmounted. The Navy was agreeable to his plan and the place and the necessary means were now at his disposal. He next turned to the question of school organization and administration and of the repairs and improvements to the buildings at Fort Severn. In studying the problem of organization and administration the most natural thing was to turn to the Military Academy at West Point, which had its experience of over forty years to offer in the way of organization and administration. This had been pointed out to him by the report of the Board of Examiners. So Professor Lockwood was sent back to his Alma Mater, in July, 1845, by Bancroft, to study West Point's improvements in methods and organization.

Commander Franklin Buchanan, well known in the Navy for his discipline and determination, as well as for his ability to organize, was selected by Secretary Bancroft to be the Superintendent of the Naval School. . . . *

Buchanan's success . . . was due not only to his ability to organize an institution revolutionizing naval education and to administer it by wise disciplinary restraints through the first period of its trying infancy; but also to his having an unusually capable faculty and to his creating at the School an effective spirit of harmony. Thus was laid the firm and lasting foundation of the present Naval Academy.

Editor's Note

*As originally published in 1929, this article ran more than eleven thousand words and contains an amazing amount of detail about the early days of the Naval Academy, but it is too long to include here in its entirety and has therefore been abridged.

2 "The First Academic Staff"

Charles Lee Lewis, Henry Francis Sturdy,
and Louis Harrison Bolander

U.S. Naval Institute *Proceedings*
(October 1935): 1389–1403

THE EARLY SUCCESS of the United States Naval Academy and the constant effort to attain higher standards, that has continued to this date, are in a large measure due to the first Academic Staff and the precedents set under the very effective leadership of Commander Franklin Buchanan, U.S. Navy, who became Superintendent with the founding of the Naval Academy on October 10, 1845. Assisting him was a very able and enthusiastic group—the first Academic Staff:

Commander Franklin Buchanan, U.S. Navy, Superintendent.
Lieutenant J. H. Ward, U.S. Navy, Executive and Instructor in Gunnery and Steam.
Professor W. Chauvenet, Instructor in Mathematics and Navigation.
Professor H. H. Lockwood, Instructor in Natural Philosophy.
Professor A. N. Girault, Instructor in French.
Chaplain G. Jones, U.S. Navy, Instructor in English.
Surgeon J. A. Lockwood, U.S. Navy, Instructor in Chemistry.
Passed Midshipman S. Marcy, U.S. Navy, Assistant Instructor in Mathematics.

No description of the Naval Academy would be complete without an account of the lives of these men who have so definitely left their stamp on the Naval Academy.

Franklin Buchanan

Franklin Buchanan was born September 17, 1800, in Baltimore, Maryland, at "Auchentorlie," the home of his father, Dr. George Buchanan, the son of a distinguished Scotch physician who had come to Maryland in 1723. Young Franklin Buchanan's mother was Laetitia McKean, daughter of the Pennsylvania "Signer," Thomas McKean, of Scotch-Irish ancestry. On January 28, 1815, Franklin became a midshipman at the age of fourteen, and saw service first on the *Java*, under the command of Commodore Oliver Hazard Perry. He spent the first 5 years of his naval career cruising in various ships, chiefly in the Mediterranean. He then secured a furlough of 15 months and went as second officer on a merchant vessel on a voyage to China. Back home again in active naval service, he spent several years in the Caribbean in Commodore David Porter's squadron and in the Natchez, under command of Master Commandant George Budd in their successful operations against the pirates of the West Indies, where the hurricanes and the yellow fever were even more dangerous enemies than the sea rovers. Again on leave in the summer of 1825, Buchanan, though only a young lieutenant 25 years old, sailed the frigate *Baltimore* of 64 guns, recently built in the city of Baltimore for the Brazilian Navy, safely through a severe storm and delivered the ship into the hands of representatives of Emperor Dom Pedro.

Then came more cruising in the Mediterranean, first in the *Constellation*, commanded by Captain A. S. Wadsworth, uncle of the poet Henry Wadsworth Longfellow, and a little later in the ship of the line *Delaware*, a crack ship commanded by Captain Henry E. Ballard. While attached to the latter vessel, Buchanan in company with the other officers was entertained at dinner in Paris by King Louis Philippe. Among these other officers were Charles S. Stewart, the famous chaplain, Andrew H. Foote, and Sidney Smith Lee, brother to Robert E. Lee. Returning home in the old frigate *United States*, Buchanan was married on February 19, 1835, to Anne Catherine Lloyd, daughter of Governor Edward Lloyd, of Wye House, and niece of Francis Scott Key. After a tour of shore duty during which he tested ordnance at Philadelphia and commanded the receiving ship at Baltimore, he went to sea as flag lieutenant on the *Constitution*, flagship of the Pacific Squadron based at Callao, Peru, under the command of Commodore Alexander Claxton. After returning home on the sloop of war *Falmouth*, he was ordered as second in command to Captain William D. Salter to the steam frigate *Mississippi*, one of the new show vessels of that day. On December 17, 1842, Buchanan, having been promoted to the rank of commander the year previous, September 8, 1841, was given his first independent command in the Navy, the sloop *Vincennes*. In her he patrolled the Caribbean for two years on the lookout for pirates and slavers, at the same time helping to keep his government in touch with affairs in Mexico and in the new Republic of Texas. In Galveston Harbor, he assisted two British merchantmen in danger of shipwreck, and for this service received the official thanks of Great Britain.

When Secretary of the Navy Bancroft began to take steps towards establishing a naval school, Buchanan among other officers was asked to assist in the selection of a site, and after Annapolis was chosen the Secretary appointed him, on August 14, 1845, to be the first superintendent of the new school. At the request of Bancroft, he submitted a detailed plan for the organization of the Naval School, as it was first called, and this plan with some slight changes by the Secretary was approved on August 28 following. For this new duty, Buchanan was admirably suited, as he was known throughout the Navy as a most able disciplinarian and a cultured gentleman, and both he and his wife were well known and most highly esteemed in Annapolis. With the formal opening of the school on October 10, 1845, he began to establish the high standards of discipline and efficiency for which the Naval Academy has become famous. In his annual report for the year 1845, Bancroft commended Buchanan's "precision and sound judgment" and "his wise adaptation of simple and moderate means to a great and noble end." Buchanan served as Superintendent until his detachment on March 2, 1847, after renewed applications for active service in the War with Mexico. Edward Chauncey Marshall, wrote:[1]

> All parties of that day, the Secretary of the Navy, the public journalists, and others bear testimony to the skill, ability, and success with which he discharged the difficult duties of his office.

Although the sloop of war *Germantown*, which was placed under Buchanan's command, arrived in Mexican waters too late to participate in the capture of Vera Cruz, she was able to join Commodore Matthew Calbraith Perry's squadron in the successful expeditions against Tuxpan and Tabasco, and Buchanan remained on duty on the Mexican coast until peace was signed on February 2, 1848. After a period of shore duty, most of which was spent in command of the Baltimore *Rendezvous*, he was appointed in 1852 to the command of the steam frigate *Susquehanna*, the flagship of Commodore Perry's squadron in the famous expedition to Japan. When after patient negotiations with the Japanese, the President's letter was at last, on July 14, 1853, ceremoniously presented at Uraga to the personal representatives of the Emperor, Buchanan, who was in charge of the landing of the American naval escort, had the unique distinction of being the first to set foot on Japanese soil. He later took a prominent part in the negotiations which led to the opening of Japanese ports to American commerce. During the expedition, the *Susquehanna*, on special service in Chinese waters, carried the American commissioner up the Yangtze-kiang to look after American interests during the Taiping Rebellion. And returning to the United States by way of Honolulu, San Francisco, and Cape Horn, this vessel, still under Buchanan's command, was the first steam warship to cross the Pacific Ocean.

After serving as a member of the Board of Officers to Promote the Efficiency of the Navy, Buchanan was placed in command of the Washington Navy Yard, meanwhile having been promoted to captain on September 14, 1855. Under the impression that Maryland would secede from the Union, he resigned from the Navy on April 22, 1861; but soon thereafter, becoming convinced that there would be a reconciliation between the North and the South, he wrote to the Navy Department requesting to withdraw his resignation. On May 14, 1861, however, he was "dismissed" from the Service. Making his way then to Richmond, Virginia, he joined the Confederate States Navy, in which he received the rank of captain on September 5, 1861. He served as Chief of the Bureau of Orders and Detail until February 24 of the following year, when he was placed in command of the Chesapeake Bay Squadron with his flag on the reconstructed U.S.S. *Merrimac*, renamed the C.S.S. *Virginia*. On March 8, Buchanan surprised the Union squadron in Hampton Roads, and destroyed the frigate *Congress*, on which his brother McKean was purser, the sloop of war *Cumberland*, and three small steamers. Having received a wound in the right thigh, inflicted by a Minie ball from the shore batteries during the engagement, he was prevented from commanding his ironclad in the renowned *Monitor-Merrimac* engagement on the following day. On August 26, 1862, he was promoted for gallant and meritorious conduct to admiral, thus becoming the ranking officer in the Confederate States Navy. His next, and last, command was that of the naval forces at Mobile. In the Battle of Mobile Bay on August 5, 1864, he commanded the Confederate Squadron, his flagship being the ram *Tennessee*. His smaller ships having been captured or driven to cover, "Old Buck" made a heroic single-handed attack against Farragut's entire fleet. In the furious engagement, the jamming of the *Tennessee's* rudder chain rendered the vessel unmanageable, and this together with other injuries forced her to surrender. Her commander, seriously wounded again in the right leg, remained a prisoner of war until exchanged in February, 1865.

Returning to his home, "The Rest," in Talbot County, Maryland, he became President of the Maryland Agricultural College from September, 1868, to June, 1869. Then, after spending about a year in Mobile where he was Secretary of the Alabama Branch of the Life Insurance Company of America, he returned to his Maryland home and family, where he died on May 11, 1874. He was buried in the cemetery of the Lloyd family at Wye House, about 4 miles distant from "The Rest." Of his nine children, eight daughters and one son, only one daughter, Mrs. Elizabeth Tayloe Sullivan, of Baltimore, now survives.

Note
1. *History of the United States Naval Academy*, pp. 87–88.

James Harmon Ward

"Sir, You are hereby notified that your service will be required at Annapolis, Md. in October next in connection with the Naval School about to be established at that place. I am, Respectfully yours, Geo. Bancroft." This terse note written on August 14, 1845, was the first intimation to Lieutenant James Harmon Ward that he had been chosen as an instructor in the projected Naval School at Annapolis. That the Secretary should select him from among the 327 officers of his grade is not difficult to understand. Park Benjamin, the historian of the Naval Academy, says that Ward "had an accomplished reputation as one of the best-educated officers in the Navy." When only 17 years old, he was graduated from the Military Academy at Norwich, Vermont, but before graduation he was given an appointment as a midshipman in the Navy, and sailed to the Mediterranean aboard the *Constitution* where he spent 4 years. The scientific achievement of his day and the possibilities for human progress through the increased use of steam fascinated him and, on his return to the United States, he applied for and was given a year's leave of absence from the Navy which he spent at Washington, now Trinity College, Hartford, Connecticut, in scientific study.

Though his sea service for the next 15 years was almost continuous and often of the most arduous character, he applied every possible moment to the study of gunnery, naval tactics, the history of his chosen profession, and what was known of the pure science of his day. He expressed his aim in these words:

If we would be fit for place, and in time to succeed those officers who have built up a glorious reputation for the Navy, we must have the knowledge, and have it too with familiarity, get it how we will.

In the winter of 1844, he gave a series of popular lectures at the old Naval School in Philadelphia, that attracted wide attention. These lectures he published later as an *Elementary Course of Instruction on Ordnance and Gunnery for Midshipmen*. In them he urged midshipmen to adopt for themselves a systematic course in self-culture, and advocated vigorously a better system of naval education for young naval officers.

He was greatly pleased with his appointment as an instructor at the new Naval School. He moved at once to Annapolis with his wife and children and entered upon his duties with enthusiasm. A month before the opening of the School, he had planned for a Library and had submitted to Commander Buchanan a list of books on ordnance and gunnery. That list was in turn sent to Secretary Bancroft who approved their purchase, "Provided that the whole cost does not exceed one hundred dollars."

When the School opened in October, 1845, he was appointed Executive Officer, a post not designated as Commandant of Midshipmen until July 1, 1850, three years after his departure from the School. He was also made instructor in gunnery and the use of steam, subjects which he was eminently well fitted to teach. In addition he was made President of the Academic Board, where he and Girault, both sincere men of most positive opinions, soon clashed. To keep the peace, the Superintendent was drawn into the work of the Board, finally becoming its presiding officer. Ward's forceful, energetic character, his devotion to the Service, as well as his high professional attainments, made a lasting impression on the School.

Ward's career, after he left the School, was most distinguished. In 1847, while the Mexican War was in progress, he was detached and given command of the *Cumberland,* Commodore Perry's flagship. While attempting to land on Tuxpan Reef, his boat was overturned, and he narrowly escaped drowning. Later, while in command of the *Jamestown* on the coast of Africa, he wrote his *Manual of Naval Tactics,* the demand for which was so great that the fourth edition had to be published and was used as a textbook at the Naval Academy. He also wrote a popular treatise on steam, called *Steam for the Million,* which enjoyed great popularity and ran into three editions.

Early in 1861 when Fort Sumter was fired on, Gideon Welles, Secretary of the Navy, called Ward to Washington to assist in preparing plans for the relief of the fort. He volunteered to command a rescue expedition, but General Scott convinced him that the undertaking would be futile and it was abandoned. He was then given charge of the water communications of the Capital and organized a small fleet, known as the Potomac Flotilla, to keep open a line of communications on the Potomac and to prevent the Confederates from crossing the river. In an attempt to dislodge a Confederate battery at Matthias Point on June 27, 1861, he, while in the act of pointing a gun, was killed by a sharpshooter. Commander Ward was the first Union naval officer to be killed in the Civil War.

William Chauvenet

William Chauvenet was the son of William Marc Chauvenet, a native of Narbonne, France, who came to Boston after the fall of Napoleon under whom he had served. There he married Mary B. Kerr and then moved to Milford, Pennsylvania, where his son and only child was born on May 24, 1820. Young William attended Doctor Samuel Jones's private school in Philadelphia where the family had again moved. The lad showed such marked ability in his studies that Jones strongly advised his father to send him to Yale College. He entered that college at the age of 16 and was graduated in 1840 with high honors in the classics and mathematics. He had been a frequent contributor to the college paper and had been the pianist of the Beethoven Society, having inherited great musical talent from his father. After graduation he assisted Professor Alexander Dallas Bache, President of Cirard College in Philadelphia, in observations on magnetism.

In 1841, he was married to Catherine Hemple of Philadelphia, and the same year was appointed a professor of mathematics in the United States Navy, serving first on the U.S.S. *Mississippi*. The following year he was placed in charge of the school organized for midshipmen who were preparing for examinations for promotion, which had been established at the Naval Asylum, an institution in Philadelphia for veteran seamen. Chauvenet attempted in vain to convert this "cram school" into a real naval school; on August 14, 1845, however, he was appointed to an instructorship in mathematics and navigation in the newly established Naval School at Annapolis, to the organization of which he made particularly valuable contributions. He was largely instrumental in the extension of the course of study from two to four years when the school was completely reorganized in 1850. In his department he offered inducement to postgraduate study by equipping an astronomical observatory, and in 1853, a separate Department of Astronomy and Navigation was established with him at its head. He probably did more than anyone to establish the Naval Academy on a firm scientific basis.

In 1859, Chauvenet was offered the position of Professor of Astronomy and Natural Philosophy at Yale and a similar position at Washington University, recently established at St. Louis. He accepted the latter offer, and in 1862 he was elected Chancellor of the university. The institution grew and prospered under his administration which ended in 1869 when he was compelled to resign on account of ill health. He died the following year on December 13, at St. Paul, Minnesota, and was buried in Bellefontaine Cemetery, St. Louis. In religion, he was a believer in the doctrines of Swedenborg.

In addition to numerous articles on astronomical and mathematical subjects, Chauvenet published several textbooks. His first was a small volume of 92 pages on the *Binomial Theorem and Logarithms for the Use of the Midshipmen at the Naval School, Philadelphia* (1843). His *Treatise on Plane and Spherical Trigonometry* appeared in 1850, and in 18l63 his greatest work, entitled *A Manual of Spherical and Practical Astronomy*, which had a great reputation in Europe as well as in the United States. His last work, *A Treatise on Elementary Geometry with Introduction to Modern Geometry* was published in the year 1870.

Chauvenet was a member of the American Philosophical Society and of the American Academy of Arts and Sciences, and was one of the incorporators of the National Academy of Sciences, of which he became vice president in 1868. He was president of the American Association for the Advancement of Science at the time of his death. On July 31, 1916, a memorial tablet in Chauvenet's honor was placed in Mahan Hall, United States Naval Academy, and in 1925 the Mathematical Association of America honored his memory by establishing "The Chauvenet Prize for Mathematical Exposition," which is awarded every five years.

Henry Hayes Lockwood

Among the foundational builders of the Naval Academy, Henry Hayes Lockwood stands out conspicuously. His initiative, his keen perception of the midshipmen's needs for military organization, training, and discipline, and his previous training and experience made him especially well-fitted for the task to which he also brought the necessary traits of character and intellect. He was pre-eminently a teacher.

Born on a farm in Kent County, Delaware, on August 17, in the last year of the War of 1812, the son of William Kirkley and Mary Hayes Lockwood, he was brought up under Quaker influences. He received his early education in a boy's school, in Dover, where he said all the boys were thrashed, as a matter of discipline, the first thing every morning. He attended Dickinson College and entered West Point, from which he graduated in 1836, being commissioned a lieutenant and assigned to the Second Artillery. It was this military training and discipline that he received at West Point as a cadet, as well as his active military experience in the field during the 1836–37 campaign of the Second Seminole War in Florida, that helped to make him one of the outstanding leaders in the first Naval Academy faculty.

Finding life in the Army, with its slow promotion, not to his taste, he resigned his commission in September, 1837, and returned to Delaware, where, for the next four years, he actively pursued the occupation of farming. These four years, with his boyhood days spent on the farm, instilled in him a love for the country, which in later years found expression in his fondness for walking and driving, and in his hobby for gardening, his advice often being sought on horticultural problems. During his long tour of duty at the Academy, he even acquired a farm on the outskirts of Annapolis, along the shores of Back Creek. This early country influence was shown not only in his well-built frame and vigorous constitution but also in that typically rural characteristic, "unfailing hospitality," for his "latch-string was always out." His early surroundings with their Quaker atmosphere undoubtedly helped to develop in him such of his outstanding traits, as tenderness, kindness, and generosity, both to friends and to foes, so well exemplified in his execution of orders during his Civil War service. Though of rather stern countenance, he possessed extreme simplicity and an unassuming manner, often insisting in his later years upon wearing his wide-brimmed, garden hat while driving down town in Washington.

Urged by his brother, John A. Lockwood, then a surgeon in the Navy and later assigned to the Naval Academy as its first surgeon, not to waste his brains and talents on the farm, he became a professor of mathematics in the Navy in 1841. He was sent to sea in the frigate *United States* for her famous cruise to the west coast, in the squadron under the command of Commodore Thomas ap. Catesby Jones. Not only did he show, through his success in instructing the midshipmen aboard ship, that his genius lay in teaching but he also gave effective proof of his diversity of accomplishments through his service as adjutant of the landing forces from the *United States* in the premature capture of Monterey in 1842. About a year before the founding of the Naval Academy, he was assigned to the Naval Asylum School where he assisted Professor Chauvenet in mathematics and navigation, and Lieutenant Ward in gunnery, thus early showing the "multiplicity of his attainments," as noted by Park Benjamin, "and the thoroughness with which he mastered all of them." From there he was transferred in 1845 to assist in the establishment and organization of the Naval School at Annapolis.

He was head of the Department of Natural Philosophy from 1845 to 1850 and, in addition, was put in charge of the Department of Gunnery from 1848 to 1850. He was head of the Department of Gunnery and Infantry Tactics from 1850 to 1855, and of Field Artillery and Infantry Tactics from 1856 to 1861. He conducted the first drill in the manual at arms and in infantry tactics as well as introducing field artillery drill. For these drills he wrote an official manual, adapting for naval purposes the Army exercises. When the Naval School was reorganized as the Naval Academy in 1850 he was put in charge of all formations. In 1846, besides the work of his own Department, he was assigned to teach astronomy and mathematics. In 1848, he was commissioned as a member of the Corps of Professors of Mathematics, which he and Chauvenet helped to have instituted. He was sent on the first practice cruise as the gunnery officer, his midshipmen gun crews making a notable record. In addition to his "multiplicity of attainments," he also possessed a high sense of duty and service. In August, 1846, he wrote from Annapolis to his betrothed, Miss Anna Booth, the daughter of Judge Booth, of Delaware, in regard to a planned honeymoon in Kent County, Delaware, and Philadelphia after their wedding on October second:

I must spend the month of October here. My course of Lectures
will commence at once, and duty to Govt. demands of me my
attention and most strenuous efforts.

When the Civil War broke out, he felt that he could better serve the
country by rejoining the Army. So he accepted in 1861 the appointment
from his native state as the colonel of the First Regiment of Delaware
Volunteers, being given special leave by the Navy Department. Promoted
to brigadier general of volunteers in August, 1861, he served "with high
distinction." He was at the head of an expedition to the Eastern Shore of
Maryland and Virginia. He was stationed at Point Lookout and Harper's
Ferry, and commanded a brigade at the Battle of Gettysburg. He was
then put in charge of the Middle Department, with headquarters at Baltimore, and in the spring and early summer of 1864 he took part in the
Virginia campaigns.

Refusing a permanent commission in the Army, he was mustered
out in August, 1865, and returned to the Naval Academy, as Head of
the Department of Natural and Experimental Philosophy from 1866 to
1869. He made constructive improvements in the courses, but, in 1869,
he was displaced by Lieutenant Commander W. T. Sampson. For a few
weeks in 1870 he was in charge of the Department of Mathematics and
was then ordered to the Naval Observatory at Washington. It was most
unfortunate that the Naval Academy should have been deprived of the
invaluable services of such a proved and experienced teacher, so eminently fitted for the special character of teaching needed at Annapolis
and with years of effective intellectual power still ahead of him. He had
rendered unique and constructive service to his country and had strik-
ingly illustrated the effectiveness of character in leadership. His ideals
were of the highest, both spiritual and mundane, with strong religious
convictions, devoid of any desire for mere wealth. He wrote to Miss Booth
in June, 1845:

Wealth I never expect or particularly desire. A comfortable main-
tenance I intend to have—cheerful content I propose as the goal
of life.

And again he wrote during the same period:

I hope I am not ungrateful to our Heavenly Father for such bless-
ings I am unworthy to give language to my sentiments towards
the Giver of every good & perfect gift.

He was retired from active duty in 1876 with the relative rank of
commodore but was always known as General Lockwood. Until two
years before his death, on December 7, 1899, at the age of 85, he still
exercised actively, taking long daily walks. His spirit of faithful and constructive service, though unmarked by any memorial at the Academy,
still lives as an inspiration for those of to-day and of the future in the
service of God and the nation.

Arsene N. Girault

His full name was Arsene Napoleon Alexandre Girault de San Fargeau.
Of the entire faculty of the Naval School that assembled at Annapolis in
October, 1845, he was the only man of foreign birth, for he was born
in Troyes, France, a year after the turn of the century. His father had
been an army contractor under the regime of Napoleon, had amassed a
considerable fortune, and was able to give his son a good classical education. However, under Louis XVIII he lost nearly everything, due to the
cancellation of his contracts by the government and the failure of his
banker in Paris. He died in 1819 leaving his wife and children in strait-
ened circumstances.

Estranged from his unsympathetic mother and disliking the business
to which she had apprenticed him, the son at the age of 24 sailed for the
United States, seeking to better his fortunes. He landed in America on

June 10, 1826, and within three weeks had secured a position in Phila-delphia as a teacher of Latin and French in a private school. A year later he joined the staff of the Mantua Classical and Military Academy near Philadelphia. On August 15, 1829, he left Mantua to return to Phila-delphia where he gave private lessons in French and Latin. To assist his pupils in their studies, he published a number of works on the study and teaching of French that brought him wide recognition. His *Colloquial and Grammatical Exercises in French*, later known as the *French Stu-dents' Manual*, ran into eight editions and was adopted as a textbook at the Naval School, as was his *Vie de Washington*, a publication that ran into twenty-four editions. He also wrote a *French Guide; Recreations, Instructive and Amusing;* and *Recueil Dramatique, or Select Dramatic Pieces.*

In 1836, three years after becoming a naturalized American citizen, he founded the Spring-Villa Seminary for young ladies at Bordentown, New Jersey. The land and buildings for his seminary were purchased from his friend, Count Survilliers, better known as Joseph Bonaparte, the elder brother of Napoleon and one-time King of Spain. He conducted this school with considerable success until November, 1842, when he was obliged, for financial reasons, to close its doors. The next spring he moved to Washington where he gave lessons in Spanish and French.

When Secretary George Bancroft was planning his Naval School, Girault was teaching in Baltimore. He was recommended to Commander Buchanan by "learned gentlemen in whom I have great confidence," as a suitable person to become a "Professor of the French Language at the Naval School." Buchanan in turn on September 3, 1845, recommended him to the Secretary. The following day Girault called on Bancroft and was offered the position of instructor in French at the Naval School to be opened the next month at Annapolis. This offer he accepted at once. He received his orders, dated September 27, to report to Commander Buchanan on October 1, "as temporary Agent of the Navy for teaching French." His salary was to be $1,200 per year.

On November 4, three weeks after the opening of the School, the Superintendent wrote Mr. Bancroft that the "importance of his services has been felt and appreciated by the students; his energy, zeal, and talent for teaching the French language, combined with his gentlemanly deportment, have gained for him the respect of all attached to the institution."

He soon had occasion to reprimand a midshipman in his classroom for insolent conduct. The matter was reported to Bancroft with Commander Buchanan fully supporting Girault. The midshipman was severely rebuked by the Secretary.

As a member of the Academic Board, he took an active part in its work and, two years after the opening of the School, recommended the adoption of a system of daily prayers, a practice that has continued to this day. Eleven days after the founding of the Corps of Mathematics, he received his commission as a "Professor of Mathematics," dated August 14, 1848. Though he was ever after listed as a "Professor of Mathematics," he never taught mathematics but continued to teach his native tongue.

In 1850, the Department of Modern Languages was founded, and included French and Spanish. In November, 1851, the two languages were separated and Professor E. A. Roget became Head of the Department of Spanish. Girault remained in charge of the French Department until February, 1866, when he left the institution, after an unbroken service of over 20 years. He was placed on the retired list with the rank of commander on December 25 1863, having reached the age of 62, but continued as Head of his Department for more than two years, when he was succeeded by Professor L. V. Dovilliers.

Professor Girault took an active part in the life of Annapolis. Almost immediately after coming to the city to live, he became interested in the founding of the Presbyterian Church, which was organized May 2, 1846. Girault was elected its first Elder and Clerk of Session, offices that he held for 13 years. He was of a deeply religious nature and was devoted to the success of the new Academy. His long service with it made a lasting impression on the institution. His son, Joseph Bonaparte, was connected with the Midshipmen's Commissary for more than 42 years.

After giving up active work, Professor Girault removed to New Brunswick, New Jersey, where he died May 2, 1874.

George Jones

George Jones, the youngest son of Robert and Elizabeth (Dunnman) Jones, was born on a farm near York, Pennsylvania, on July 30, 1800. He was graduated from Yale College in 1823, and three years later was awarded the A.M. degree. After teaching two years in Washington where he organized a school, he became secretary to Commodore Charles Morris, in command of the *Brandywine*, and also a teacher of navigation to the midshipmen attached to that ship, among whom was Matthew Fontaine Maury. After the *Brandywine* bore Lafayette back to France following his historic visit to the United States, she sailed to the Mediterranean where Jones was transferred to the *Constitution*, then under the command of Captain D. T. Patterson. An interesting account of the cruise of this famous frigate to important Mediterranean ports was written by Jones in the form of 67 letters, published under the title of *Sketches of Naval Life* (1829).

Upon his return to the United States in 1828, Jones became a tutor at Yale for two years and then, after being ordained a deacon in the Episcopal Church by Bishop Brownell at Hartford, Connecticut, on January 16, 1831, he served as rector of the Episcopal Church at Middletown, Connecticut. After a year, however, he was forced to give up this position on account of poor health and to seek employment in the open air in Indiana. He then decided to re-enter the Naval Service, and in 1832 he was able to accept Commodore Patterson's invitation to become acting chaplain on the frigate *United States*, then flagship of the Mediterranean Squadron. In that vessel and in the *Delaware*, to which Commodore Patterson and he were transferred in March, 1834, he made another extensive cruise in the Mediterranean, an account of which he wrote under the title of *Excursions to Cairo, Jerusalem, Damascus, and Balbec*. This was published in 1836, the same year he returned to the United States, having previously been commissioned chaplain on April 20, 1833.

He served for four years at the Norfolk Navy Yard, and for five years on the frigates *Macedonian*, *Columbus*, *Constitution*, and *Brandywine* in turn, doing effective temperance work among the crews. He also became interested in the establishment of a naval school and wrote an appeal for such an institution which was published in the *Naval Magazine*, corresponded with various naval officers, and had an interview with Secretary of the Navy Upshur in Washington on the subject. This was probably the chief reason why, on his return from a cruise to China in September, 1845, he was ordered to the Naval School, then only recently established at Annapolis. The Department of English Studies, of which he was in a real sense given full charge, being the only member thereof, comprised also history and geography as well as English. Jones successfully discharged the duties of this position until 1850 when, a chaplaincy having been established at the Naval School at its reorganization in October of that year, he was appointed the first Chaplain of the renamed United States Naval Academy.

In 1852, Commodore Matthew C. Perry applied for Jones's services, declaring that he "could be useful to him" in his Expedition to Japan. After the cruise came to a successful close, Jones was ordered by Perry to remain in New York to assist in preparing the official report of the expedition, his particular contribution being the "Observations of the Zodiacal Light," to be found in Vol. III of the report. Then, obtaining leave of absence for a year, he went to Quito, Ecuador, where he spent 7 months making observations to confirm his theory that this astronomical phenomenon is caused by a nebulous ring around the earth.

Upon his return home in the spring of 1857, he again was appointed to be Chaplain of the Naval Academy. After this service of 4 years and a short tour of duty on the *Minnesota* during the Civil War, he was retired for age in July, 1862. Afterwards during the war he volunteered his services as chaplain and nurse in the Army hospitals in Washington and at Gettysburg. After retirement he also published two other books, *Life-Scenes from the Four Gospels* (1865) and *Life-Scenes from the Old Testament* (1868), pioneer attempts to make vividly real and life-like the scenes of the Bible. Jones died at the United States Naval Asylum in Philadelphia on January 22, 1870, about 5 years after the death of his wife, Mary Amelia, who was the oldest daughter of Gold S. Silliman, Brooklyn, New York.

John Alexander Lockwood

John Alexander Lockwood, elder brother of Professor Henry Hayes Lockwood, was graduated from the Medical School of Dickinson College, Carlisle, Pennsylvania, and in 1832 was commissioned as an assistant surgeon in the United States Navy. Though a native of Delaware, being born there in 1811, he was descended from one of the earliest Massachusetts settlers, Richard Lockwood, who came from England and landed at Watertown in 1632. His wife, Julia McLane, was also from Delaware. No doubt Surgeon Lockwood's attraction to the Navy was due, in part, to his father's service in the Navy as a midshipman, in 1809 and 1810. He was not Secretary Bancroft's first choice but was only ordered to Annapolis to be the surgeon and the professor of chemistry at the Naval School, after Surgeon Du Barry had declined that post. He was considered to have been an able doctor. He had a good mind, with a literary bent.

Soon after the Naval School opened, he fitted up a room as a dispensary and later converted an adjoining room as a sick bay, with a woman nurse. Her time was so taken up, however, with nursing Acting Midshipman Grundy during his protracted illness, that Surgeon Lockwood requested that a hospital steward be assigned to the School to look after the midshipmen in sick bay. Though, besides the illness of Grundy, one midshipman had to be sent to Philadelphia to a hospital and another one home to be nursed, the Superintendent reported to the Secretary that the health of those at the School was good. The need for a small hospital became so apparent by the end of the first year that one was included in Buchanan's building program. Surgeon Lockwood was sent to Baltimore in December, 1846, to obtain the necessary furniture for this new hospital, which was then nearing completion.

Besides his medical care of those stationed at the Naval School, he taught chemistry, being head of that Department. After Lieutenant Ward's detachment, steam was assigned to him as well; later he also lectured in international law. He gave Commander Buchanan effective co-operation in the disciplinary policy at the School and was apparently quick to note the effects of dissipation upon the health of the midshipmen. It is said that he, himself, considered "his most valuable service to the Navy" to have been the publication of his book *Flogging in the Navy*.

He remained at the Naval School until December, 1849, when he was detached and shortly after sent out for service in the East India and Mediterranean squadrons. After those tours of duty, ending in July, 1858, he was put in charge of the Naval Hospital at the New York Navy Yard, in Brooklyn. After serving, during the Civil War, as Fleet Surgeon of the Pacific Squadron, he resigned from the Navy. He went to California to live, and after remaining there awhile be moved to England until his death in 1900.

Samuel Marcy

Passed Midshipman Samuel Marcy was a representative of the highest type of young officer in the Navy in 1845. He was the ideal type to have in contact with the youngsters just entering the Service and was also a stimulating example for those midshipmen who, having been in the Service for the requisite five years, were now preparing themselves for promotion. His educational groundwork before entering the Service as a midshipman, at the age of 18, was very sound, and his home background gave him that necessary refinement and character so essential for the real leader in any profession. His father was the American statesman and patriot Lamed Marcy, who served in the War of 1812, and who held the public offices of Senator from New York, Governor of New York, and of both Secretary of War and Secretary of State of the United States. The transfer of Fort Severn from the jurisdiction of the Army to that of the Navy was undoubtedly brought about, in part at least, by young Marcy whose year's duty at the Naval Asylum School must have conclusively shown to him the need for a regularly organized naval school.

The fact that his father at that time was the Secretary of War gave him an unusual opportunity to promote the transfer. Not only that but it also enabled him to go to West Point under the most favorable conditions to study its system of organization, administration, and studies.

Though entering the Navy in 1838, before there was in existence any system of education for the midshipmen, he took advantage of his opportunities for self-development. His notes show a thoroughness of detail and a desire for mastery. This is especially true in his study of seamanship which afterwards enabled him to assist Stephen B. Luce very materially, in the writing of his treatise on that subject and to contribute most effectively in laying the foundation of the course in seamanship, when it was introduced in the reorganization of the School in 1850–51. His studies and interest in naval tactics and in gunnery, with his well-executed sketches and notes on naval construction, gave him a breadth of view and a well-rounded professional education that made him ideally fitted as an instructor for midshipmen at the Academy.

This especially desirable fitness was apparently appreciated by the authorities, for, in the first 16 years of the Naval Academy's existence, he was sent there for three separate tours of duty. The first two of these tours were in the very critical stages of the Academy's development. The first was at the very beginning of the year 1845–46, when he was assigned as assistant instructor in mathematics, under Professor Chauvenet. The second was at the time of reorganization in 1850–51, when he was again assistant in mathematics and also assistant to the Commandant, a newly created post. At this period he was kept at the Academy for about 4 years and must have been an invaluable officer for the organization of the just-begun summer practice cruises. The third, which concluded his work at the Academy, found him again as assistant to the Commandant, for the period of about 3 years, just preceding the outbreak of the Civil War. His work at the Academy was rendered much more effective by his keeping constantly abreast of the times and in touch with the contemporary professional developments both at home and abroad. This broadening of his horizon was greatly augmented by his linguistic ability, which gave him the great advantage of being able to follow the ideas in the naval profession abroad.

Whether or not his studious habits and inclinations made the environment of St. John's College especially attractive may never be known, but it seems very suitable that he should have married Miss Eliza Humphreys, the daughter of Dr. Hector Humphreys, the President of St. John's and a cousin of the famous naval constructor, Joshua Humphreys. Professor Lockwood, perhaps, has left us the most accurate contemporary picture of young Marcy as a passed midshipman in 1845: "He is a young man, passed midshipman, modest, studious and very gentlemanly."

It seems most unfortunate that such an outstanding officer should have been killed in the prime of life, just when his positions of command would have enabled him to indoctrinate others with the spirit of sound constructive leadership. This seems especially so as his death, which occurred at the Southeast Pass of the Mississippi, in January, 1862, was brought about by the carelessness of workmanship in ordnance construction. For if there was one phase of professional efficiency that marked Lieutenant Commander Marcy's career it was that of thoroughness. It was on blockade duty at the Southeast Pass, while in command of the U.S. ship *Vincennes*, that he was mortally wounded by the recoil of a boat howitzer, which he was personally firing in an attempt to destroy an abandoned barkentine which had been trying to run out of the Pass. The "bolt securing the pivot clamp to the bows of the launch drew out, in consequence of being insufficiently riveted at the navy yard."

His death, however, in the active discharge of his duty on the first line of defense of his country should be an effective example to the midshipman of today that intellectual development can only give greater and more effective power of leadership in times of national need.

3 "The New Naval Academy"

Ernest Flagg, Architect

U.S. Naval Institute *Proceedings*
(1899): 865–73

THE NAVAL ACADEMY was founded in 1845 when George Bancroft was Secretary of the Navy, and was then located where it is to-day, at Annapolis, Maryland. Some buildings connected with the military post attached to old Fort Severn were pressed into service, and from time to time other buildings were added to them. The old fort stands on the point at the mouth of the Severn river. It is a curious little round structure, having immensely thick walls and a protected entrance from the land side. In recent years a one-story wooden structure has been built on top of the old walls, and the fort now does duty as the gymnasium of the academy. Formerly the water almost washed its base, but from time to time land has been reclaimed from the river, and the structure now stands some distance inside the sea wall. Under the proposed scheme for remodeling the academy, more land will be reclaimed by extending the sea wall on the bay side out to the Port Wardens line and the fort will be thrown still further back. It is proposed to restore this little historic relic to its original appearance, and to mount upon it the old guns, in which condition it will form an interesting feature of the parade ground, and will present a striking contrast to the proposed new practice battery on the point.

From time to time the Government has acquired more land about the old reservation. One of the most important of these acquisitions was the purchase of the grounds with the mansion of the colonial governors of Maryland. The old building still exists and is used as the library of the academy. It has, however, been sadly transformed during the last hundred years. It has been shorn of its wings, in which were the slaves' quarters, the old porch has been removed from the front and replaced by one not in character with the building, and a heavy new roof has been added, which almost entirely robs the exterior of its former beauty. One roof was burned off. There seems to be no record of the time of this occurrence, but the writer, upon making an examination, found the remains of three roofs, one of which had been very much damaged by fire. The successive roofs have been built one over the other, and it is therefore hardly to be wondered at that the last one looks heavy. The proposed scheme for rebuilding contemplates the restoration of this interesting and historic relic to its original condition, and utilizing it as a residence of the commander of the place, who is known officially as the superintendent. Those who have read Richard Carvel will doubtless remember several references to this old building. When restored it will add greatly to the beauty and interest of the place.

With the exception of the governors' house, and the old fort, there are no buildings of any interest or beauty on the grounds. All are old, poorly built, and many of them are much out of repair. Some have recently been condemned as unsafe, and several have been torn down for this reason. It seems to have been the policy of the Government to build here in the poorest way, and to place the buildings wherever there was a vacant place, with absolutely no regard to the convenient and economical working of the institution. Thus, the armory, which now has one side shored to keep it from falling out, is in a most inconvenient place, almost as far from the parade ground as the limits of the yard will admit, and much time and labor are lost daily in marching and hauling guns by devious paths back and forth between it and the parade ground whenever there is a drill. The recitation buildings seem to have been located by chance, and the boat house, a part of which was condemned as unsafe within five years after it was built, is in a most inconvenient position with regard to the cadets' quarters.

In the scheme for rebuilding, it has been the endeavor to place every building in the location best adapted to it—where it will fit in most advantageously for the routine work of the institution, and most harmoniously from the artistic standpoint.

The flimsy character of the old buildings was amusingly illustrated in a story which Admiral Matthews (chairman of the committee which recommended the proposed scheme for rebuilding) told of an experience of his when a boy at the academy. One night when he and some comrades were studying in their rooms in one of the old buildings, they suddenly heard a rumbling sound, the lights were extinguished, there was a rush of cold air, then a terrible crash. One side of the building had fallen out, leaving the rooms open on the side toward the water. Fortunately the floor beams did not rest on this wall, or the admiral would probably not have been alive to tell the story. As it was, the young men found themselves sitting on a shelf in the open air. Recently one of the buildings of this same row was found to be split in two from top to bottom. The two halves seemed to be only held together by the weight of the roof, and it was necessary to rig up great spars and tie the building together with ropes before it could be taken down. In spite of the flimsy character and unsightly appearance of many of the buildings of the academy, the place is attractive, and can hardly fail to produce an agreeable impression upon the visitor. The grounds are always in the most immaculate order. The well-kept walks, fine trees, smooth lawns and beautiful outlook over the bay, all combine to make a most attractive picture and to indicate how beautiful it can be made when all its natural beauties are brought out and the blemishes removed.

The Government owns three pieces of property, comprising several hundred acres, which are more or less disconnected, but which are set apart for the purpose of the academy. The principal one of these, and where it is proposed to place all the new structures, adjoins the town of Annapolis and occupies the point which is formed by the southern bank of the Severn river, where the latter meets Chesapeake Bay. It has a frontage on the bay of about 1200 feet, and a frontage on the river of about 2400 feet. These two water-fronts form an acute angle, so that the property is wider at one end than it is at the other. This would not be so if the sea wall along the river followed the true line of the stream, for the channel of the river makes almost a right angle with the Port Wardens line along the bay side. In the scheme for rebuilding, it is intended to reclaim some part of the flats on the south side of the river by building a great pier, upon which will stand the power house, storage warehouse and steam engineering building, and to dredge out the rest of the shallow area so as to form a basin for the practice boats of the academy; the basin to be partially enclosed by piers following the true line of the river; this will square out the property and bring it almost to the form of a rectangular quadrilateral, having a breadth of 1284 feet, and a length of about 2500 feet. The basin will have a length of 1083 feet and a width of 580 feet. It is proposed to build a fine new sea wall of massive masonry along all this waterfront and around the basin.

The academy has two main entrances which stand at the head of two of the streets of the town. Another street at right angles to these runs along the wall. When one enters he faces towards the Severn river. At present the view of the river, which is very pretty here, is obstructed by a row of unsightly coal sheds and wooden buildings which line the water-front. It is proposed to remove all these and to open up a charming view of the river, with the basin in the foreground, the latter enclosed with massive sea walls of granite, its entrance flanked by stone beacons standing at the ends of the two piers which partially separate it from the river; and the shipping along the quays will produce a striking and characteristic effect. On the southerly side of the basin advantage has been taken of the natural lay of the land to broaden out the quay into a sort of semi-circular place suggestive of an amphitheatre, with concentric rows of broad steps on the banks, which represent the difference in grade between the made land of the quay and the solid ground of the campus. This place will have a length of 415 feet and a width of 250 feet. It is intended for use at out-of-door exercises. The band stand is placed at the center of the side toward the basin. A great multitude could be accommodated on the steps or gradients of the amphitheatre. The fine old trees now on the campus are to be preserved, the lawns extended toward the river, and the parade ground greatly increased by moving the sea wall on the bay side out to the Port Wardens line.

When the proposed plan is carried out the buildings will be in three main groups, one on each of the three sides of the campus, on the other side of which is the basin with its shipping. The cadets' quarters will be on the right hand side as one enters from the town, the academic buildings on the left, and the officers' houses, as at present, on a line parallel to and just inside the wall which encloses the academy grounds on the side towards the town. The cadets' quarters will stand between the campus and the parade ground. It will be flanked on one side by the boat-house and on the other side by the armory. The main floors of these two latter buildings will be at the level of the parade ground, which, being of made land, is lower than the campus. The cadets' quarters will stand on the higher level, and the difference in grade between the campus on one side and the parade grounds on the other will be made up by a stone terrace about 18 ft. high on the side towards the parade ground, so that the quarters will appear to stand on a terrace when viewed from the parade ground or from the bay.

The boat-house and armory are to be connected with the cadets' quarters by covered ways. The northwesterly end of the boat-house abuts upon the basin, and the main longitudinal axis of the building and the basin coincide.

The academic building at the other side of the campus faces the cadets' quarters; the main axes of both these buildings coincide. They will be connected by a broad avenue of trees. The academic building is flanked on one side by the physics and chemistry building, and on the other side by the steam engineering building. The latter, with the power house and general storage warehouse, form a group which will stand on the reclaimed land at the northwesterly end of the basin. The power house, which is the central building of the three, will face the boat-house at the other end of the basin. Their longitudinal axes coincide with that of the basin; his general plan, that is to say, the grouping of the buildings, and arrangement of the grounds, and the treatment of the water-front, was prepared by a commission appointed by Secretary Herbert, pursuant to a resolution adopted by the Board of Visitors to the Naval Academy of 1895, requesting the Secretary to appoint a commission "to examine and report upon the condition of the grounds and buildings and the sanitary condition of said Academy." The following extract is from the report of the Board of Visitors:

"The Board feels that the Naval Academy should be an institution second to none of its kind in the world; that it should meet every modern requirement as an institution of learning, not only as to the instruction given, but as to the conveniences and accommodation offered officers, instructors, and cadets. It feels that the present buildings are insufficient and inadequate for the purposes to which they are assigned, and that a reconstruction of buildings, grounds, and sanitation, upon the most approved modern architectural and sanitary lines, will not only be an incalculable benefit to the naval service, but a progressive step which will meet the approval of the whole country."

A commission was appointed by the Secretary of the Navy, July 5th, 1895, and consisted of Admiral (then Commodore) E.O. Matthews; Captain P.H. Cooper, U.S.N. (then superintendent of the Naval Academy);

Lieutenant-Commander E.H.C. Leutze, U.S.N.; Lieutenant-Commander A. Ross, U.S.N.; W.R. DuBose, surgeon, U.S.N.; and W.P. Potter, Lieutenant, U.S.N., recorder.

An extract from the report of this commission reads as follows:

"The Board met at this place on July 16th, 1895, and made a careful inspection of the buildings, grounds and sewerage system. After examining into the needs of the service for which the buildings were erected and the present arrangement and conditions, we find the present buildings are, with few exceptions, in very bad condition and not warranting the expense of the extensive repairs that would be needed to render them safe and serviceable, which repairs would only be temporary, and even then they are so misplaced as to be very inconvenient; others, though now in fairly good condition, will soon begin to require unending repairs, and are so misplaced as to interfere with any proper general plan.

"Owing to the extensive flats surrounding the water-front, which are either exposed at low water or very near the surface, a proper sewerage system is almost if not quite impossible under the present conditions, and the Board, looking to the permanent needs of a great and growing nation, is of the opinion that in the interest of true economy and efficiency, a plan should be adopted for the erection of substantial fireproof buildings of indestructible material, properly arranged and situated, to be convenient, healthful, and thoroughly adapted to the requirements of an institution that is to last for all time.

"Before the erection of the new structures can be commenced the Board deem it of prime importance to install a permanent sanitary sewerage system and to prepare the grounds. This can only be accomplished by raising existing ground along the water-front and filling in in other places. For that purpose, and at the same time securing sufficient depth of water-front for the handling of boats and vessels used in instruction, dredging should be commenced and a suitable sea wall built."

When the board was appointed it was directed by the Secretary of the Navy that its report be accompanied by a map of the buildings and grounds as now constituted, and also a map of the buildings and grounds as they will appear under the system to be proposed by the board.

A great deal of time, study and care were given to the preparation of this latter map or general plan. The commission met many times on the grounds and carefully considered the needs of the institution and the proper location of the new buildings. Mr. Ernest Flagg, architect, of New York, was invited to assist in the preparation of a plan which should embody the ideas of the board, and his plan was submitted with their report.

The reasons which governed in the preparation of this plan were briefly these:

The area of the grounds was thought to be too restricted. To overcome this and at the same time to deepen the water along the sea walls, it was proposed to reclaim flats which lay under water on two sides, and to obtain the necessary filling by dredging out a part of the area for a basin. By thus raising the general level and deepening the water, the difficulties in the way of the installation of a proper sewer system would also be overcome. In placing the buildings it was thought that as the institution was chiefly for the benefit of the cadets, the cadets' quarters ought to occupy the best and most commanding location on the grounds, that is to say, the site of the present superintendent's residence. There were also other weighty reasons for the selection of this location for the quarters, the most important of which was its proximity to the parade ground, which is admirably located inside the sea wall on the bay side. By placing the boat-house to the northeast of the cadets' quarters, and the armory to the southwest of it, all three of these buildings would be located in the most advantageous positions with respect to the grounds and with respect to themselves. The armory would be contiguous to the parade ground, the boat-house to the basin, and the quarters within convenient reach of each. To still further facilitate communication between these three buildings, it was determined to connect them by covered ways. It is generally necessary that the cadet should change his clothes preparatory to duties on land or water, it is therefore desirable that the quarters should be within reasonable reach of the boat-house and armory. The plan adopted accomplishes this purpose admirably.

The officers' houses were thought to be well located in their present position, and that when the cadets' quarters are placed on one side and the academic building on the other side of the square upon which they face, no more convenient location could be desired.

The old governors' mansion, which it was desired to preserve both for historical and artistic reasons, seemed to be admirably located for a residence for the superintendent, standing, as it does, at the head of the row of officers' houses. It was thought best to attach the library to the academic building, so that it should be within easy reach from the classrooms of the various departments. It was placed to the west of and adjoining the academic building, from which it is separated by enclosed courts. The physics and chemistry departments, and the department of steam engineering, each requires separate buildings; these were placed one at either side of the academic building. It was also thought desirable that the steam engineering building should be closely connected with the power house, so that power can be easily transmitted to it, and so that the apparatus of the power house itself might be used for illustration and instruction.

This disposition of the buildings not only has the advantage of bringing every building into the place most convenient for it, but also of placing them where they will produce a fine artistic effect and not interfere with the natural beauties of the place.

Although the report of the Matthews commission was presented January 16th, 1896, no action was taken by the Department until 1898. When the report was made Secretary Herbert thought that, in the then condition of the national finances, Congress would not be likely to enter upon an undertaking of such magnitude as that suggested by the Matthews board. In 1898 the recitation building was found to be unsafe, the Department concluded that something would have to be done, and Congress was asked to make an appropriation to commence the work in accordance with what was known as the "Matthews plan." Although the sum asked for was stricken out in committee, the House, upon motion of Mr. Mudd of Maryland, agreed to an amendment appropriating $1,000,000 to be applied to the erection of the boat-house, the armory, the power house and a part of the sea wall; $500,000 of this sum was not to be available until the following year. At the next session the secretary was asked for a further sum to commence work on the other buildings, and although committee again failed to include any part of the amount asked for in the bill reported to the House, Mr. Mudd again secured by amendment the appropriation of $720,000 for the work already authorized; $220,000 of this amount was rendered necessary by the determination to make all the buildings of granite instead of brick and limestone as originally contemplated. The plans had been prepared by Mr. Flagg in accordance with the Matthews report. Bids for the work were advertised for and contracts for it were finally made with P. J. Carlin & Co., of Brooklyn, N.Y. The work was commenced March 28th, 1899, and has been in progress ever since. It is expected that the buildings now under erection will be completed in about a year. The Department has asked the present Congress for upwards of $2,000,000 to continue the work upon other buildings of the plan.

"The Yard"

4

Nancy Prothro Arbuthnot

(Selection from *Guiding Lights: United States Naval Academy Monuments and Memorials*, Naval Institute Press, 2009): 2–13

. . . ALTHOUGH THE ACADEMY has changed greatly over the years since the construction of the "New Naval Academy," built between 1899 (the laying of the cornerstone of the new Armory—later Dahlgren Hall) and 1908 (the dedication of the new Chapel), the heart of the Yard retains the grand Beaux-Arts design of architect Ernest Flagg. Now, as the New Academy nears completion of the first decade of its second hundred years and a new era of growth, it is appropriate to review the Yard's architectural history.

Beginnings of a Naval School, 1800–45

The Naval School, as it was first known, came into existence in 1845. The U.S. Navy was established in 1775 (later disestablished in 1783–84, but then reestablished in 1794), but no formal institution for the training of naval officers was provided for during those periods of the active Navy. As early as 1800, however, President John Adams had suggested to Congress that such a school be started. Decades of attempts followed, including the informal shipboard training offered aboard ships such as the frigate *Guerriere* in 1821 in New York and the frigate *Java* in Norfolk, Virginia, in 1822; a training program at the Boston Navy Yard in

1833; and an educational program for midshipmen at the Philadelphia Naval Asylum in 1839. The first successful introduction of steamships into the Navy in 1837 (USS *Fulton II*, Capt. Matthew C. Perry, commanding) led to increased concern for appropriate training to run the new technology. The *Somers* incident of 1842—during which three men aboard USS *Somers*, including Midn. Philip Spencer, son of Secretary of War John Spencer, were hanged for mutiny—renewed interest in the method of appointment of midshipmen and army cadets. In 1844 William Chauvenet, a young professor of mathematics at the Naval Asylum in Philadelphia and before that a shipboard instructor, developed a comprehensive two-year curriculum for naval officer training. A year and a half later, on August 7, 1845, George Bancroft, Secretary of the Navy under President Polk, proposed a plan "to collect the midshipmen who from time to time are on shore, and give them instruction . . . in the study of mathematics, nautical astronomy, theory of morals, international law, gunnery, use of steam, the Spanish and French languages, and other branches essential . . . to the accomplishment of a naval officer."

On August 15, bypassing Congress, Bancroft arranged for the transfer of Fort Severn on the banks of the Severn River in Annapolis, Maryland, to the Department of the Navy, and moved the Naval Asylum to Annapolis. Cdr. Franklin Buchanan was placed in charge, professors were selected (among them William Chauvenet), and midshipmen received orders to report to Annapolis.

At 11:00 a.m. on Friday, October 10, 1845, Commander Buchanan, the school's first superintendent, declared the Naval School open. He read aloud Secretary Bancroft's August 7 letter of instruction to about fifty midshipmen and seven officers and civilian instructors and charged the midshipmen with new challenges. Reminding them of the "uncalculable benefit" of an education bestowed on them by the government and that "good moral character is essential" to promotion, he closed his remarks by challenging the students to a "strict compliance with all laws, orders and regulations" in the hopes that they "may be benefited by them."

The almost ten-acre grounds of the former Fort Severn on the eastern edge of Annapolis on Windmill Point, a peninsula where the Severn River joins the Annapolis Harbor, was rapidly adapted to its new use as the Naval School. Within the walls of the old fort were the circular gun battery at the tip of the peninsula, dating from 1808, and other buildings, including the commandant's quarters (a colonial mansion called Dulany House), a row of officers' quarters (later known as Buchanan Row), the quartermaster's office, a barracks, married officers' quarters, a hospital, a bakery, the sutler's shop, the blacksmith shop, and the gatehouse. The barracks was converted into classrooms and mess, and other buildings were converted to midshipmen housing.

The Early Years of the Academy, 1845–61

The late 1840s brought new land to the Academy, and the 1850s and 1860s, a new building program. Land adjacent to the Academy acquired in 1847 added six acres to the grounds. The first monument, the Mexican War Monument, was erected in 1848. An extensive construction program undertaken in 1850–54 provided new dorms, a combined laboratory-armory, a recitation hall, and a chapel. Additional land purchased in 1853 added another eleven acres to the grounds, creating space for a hospital and faculty quarters. By 1859 the population of the Academy had expanded as well to a total of fourteen civilian instructors and about the same number of officers and about eighty midshipmen. The sloop *Plymouth* was brought to the Academy and converted into a lodging and classroom facility for fourth-class midshipmen. Another construction program started in 1859 brought the demolition of several older buildings and the construction of new ones. Three permanent additions to the Yard's landscape were made: the Japanese Bell given to Commodore Perry during his expedition to Japan and donated by Perry's widow; Herndon Monument, erected in June 1860; and the Tripoli Monument, moved from the grounds of the Capitol building in Washington, D.C., to the Academy in November 1860.

The Civil War Years, 1861–65

Soon after the outbreak of civil war, the school buildings and grounds transferred to the War Department. On April 24 Superintendent Blake requested an immediate transfer of the school to Fort Adams, an unused Army post at Newport, Rhode Island, and on April 26 the battalion mustered at the Academy wharf to board *Constitution*. (By this time, a number of Southern midshipmen had resigned to support the Confederacy, which soon established its own naval academy aboard CSS *Patrick Henry*.) On April 27 Secretary of the Navy Gideon Welles approved the transfer of the Academy to Fort Adams. After delivering two companies of soldiers at the New York Navy Yard, *Constitution* departed Brooklyn on May 8 with the midshipmen and reached Newport on May 9. Meanwhile *Baltic*, which had departed Annapolis on May 5, 1861, carrying Academy officers, instructors, and families as well as instructional resources, arrived off Fort Adams on May 9, three and a half hours after *Constitution*'s arrival. Classes convened on May 13, but by July, when the Class of 1865 began reporting (altogether the official register lists two hundred midshipmen, most of whom came in September, October, and November 1861), the deteriorating facilities at Fort Adams had to be abandoned. Although Fort Adams continued to be used for training midshipmen throughout the war, classes were held in Atlantic House, which also housed the faculty and upper class while the fourth class remained quartered on *Constitution*. The Civil War years, requiring the maximum number of midshipmen to be graduated in the minimum time, presented some of the most challenging years the Academy had to face.

During these years, the Academy grounds functioned in a variety of ways from May 1861 as an Army encampment; from late 1861 to February 1862 a port of embarkation for a joint Army-Navy operation on the North Carolina coast; and from 1863 to the end of the war as an Army hospital. An eyewitness account published in the *Army and Navy Journal* in 1864 described the hospital conditions on the Academy grounds:

My eyes were struck by the view of a number of hospital tents occupying the grounds once held sacred from the footprints of anyone. Around these tents were trodden innumerable footpaths, marring the beauty of the grounds. Next came an unsightly board fence dividing the upper from the lower grounds; then came roads and pathways, made on pavements and grass plots, the crossing of which once subjected a student to demerits. . . . The fine buildings I found occupied in various ways. Most of them are used as hospitals, while other portions are given up as sutler-shops, where lager-beer, etc., is dispensed. The fine old quarters of the Superintendent are used as a billiard saloon. What a transformation from their once legitimate use. . . . Thousands of dollars will be required to restore this valuable institution to its original condition.

The Porter Vision, 1865–69

When classes reconvened at the Academy in October 1865, the grounds had been restored to something of their former state. But size was a pressing concern. Stribling Row, built to house 198 midshipmen, could not accommodate the 566 midshipmen who now enrolled. Rear Adm. David Dixon Porter, appointed on September 9, 1865, as the Academy's sixth superintendent, envisioned a great national institution and embarked on a major expansion and construction campaign. In August 1866 he first purchased the four-acre Maryland Government House and grounds. He turned the former governor's residence into the library and superintendent's office and razed the outbuildings in order to erect a new row of officers' quarters. He also acquired more land for the Academy with purchases of two separate parcels north of Dorsey (now College) Creek: the July 1868 purchase of the sixty-seven-acre Strawberry Hill, where the cemetery was established in 1869, and in May 1869, a forty-six-acre tract known as Prospect Hill (where the huge green water tower is today), where he established the hospital (a decision later known as Porter's folly). Meanwhile, in 1865 he constructed a new armory; in 1866, a hall for the Department of Steam Engineering; in 1868, a new chemistry laboratory and brick chapel (the old chapel was converted into the lyceum); and in 1869, a science building and the midshipmen's New Quarters. (The dormitories along Stribling Row, now known as the Old Quarters, were used as overflow housing.) The USS *Delaware* figurehead, now known as Tecumseh, was brought to the Academy and placed near the Lyceum sometime around 1868. USS *Santee*, first brought to the Academy as quarters for enlisted personnel and a brig for midshipmen, became a gunnery ship for the practice firing of broadsides.

The Quiet Years, 1868–96

Over the next thirty years, relatively few changes were made to the Academy grounds. The first superintendent's quarters, Dulany House, was demolished in 1883–84, and a second superintendent's house was completed there in 1886. An additional fifteen acres along the College Creek shoreline were purchased, and construction was begun on the redbrick officers' quarters on Upshur Row. Most of the older buildings were in dangerously dilapidated condition.

The Flagg Years, 1895–1908

In 1895 the Board of Visitors condemned the existing facilities and asserted that only reconstruction along modern architectural lines would raise the Academy to the level of a premier institution. The board then commissioned Ernest Flagg to develop a master plan for a new Academy.

Ernest Flagg (1857–1947), an American architect trained at the Ecole des Beaux-Arts in Paris and the architect of the Corcoran Gallery of Art (1892–97) in Washington, D.C., and the Singer Tower (1906–8) in New York City, devised a plan for a "New Naval Academy" of architectural monuments to the Navy's grand traditions. To accomplish his vision required almost complete demolition of existing buildings (with the exception of the Gate 3 gatehouses, built in 1876 and now the oldest surviving buildings in the Yard), expansion with sizable landfills along both the river and harbor shores, and buildings in monumental Beaux-Arts style, grouped in functional units: a dormitory flanked by buildings for the professional training of midshipmen in the southern part of the Yard; an "academic group" at the northern end; a chapel to provide spiritual guidance to midshipmen; an administrative building; quarters for the superintendent and faculty; and an officers' club.

The dormitory (now called Bancroft Hall), built between 1902 and 1905 to replace the Old Cadet Quarters, stands on the southeastern part of the central Yard as the centerpiece of Flagg's plan. The building's original design included the rotunda, Memorial and Smoke Halls, today's third and fourth wings—and room for expansion, which has been used to add six more wings over the years. In front of Bancroft, Tecumseh Court (T-Court) provides a wide bricked yard for midshipmen formations.

As planned for in Flagg's design, the dormitory is flanked by professional buildings—the identical facades of one building to house the gymnasium and the Department of Seamanship (now Macdonough Hall), originally abutting the shore, and the Armory (now Dahlgren Hall), housing the Department of Ordnance and Gunnery. At the end of Stribling Walk, two long parallel brick paths running from Bancroft through the central yard, Flagg placed the academic group, a set of three joined structures: Sampson Hall and Maury Hall facing each other across the open, recessed courtyard in front of the middle building with the clock tower, Mahan Hall.

Sampson originally housed the Physics and Chemistry Department and the Mathematics Department, and Maury, the English and Law Department and the Modern Languages Department. In addition to the clock tower, Mahan provided an auditorium and library. In the rear of these buildings stood Isherwood Hall, housing the Marine Engineering and Naval Construction Department and the Mechanics Department.

Sited on the highest ground in the Yard and almost midway between the dormitory and the academic group, facing east toward the Severn River, is the Chapel. Flagg modeled the Chapel on the dome of the Hotel des Invalides in Paris, originally designed by Jules Hardouin Mansart (1646–1708) to house disabled veterans, but since 1840 better known as the tomb of Napoleon Bonaparte. The Superintendent's Quarters (now called Buchanan House) sits on one side of the Chapel, and the Administration Building sits on the other.

In 1905, an officers' club was erected on Goldsborough Row, and additional officer housing was planned for Porter and Rodgers roads.

Flagg's grand plan also called for placing monuments and nautical mementos (such as cannons, anchors, ships' bells, and figureheads) around the central grounds to "assist [midshipmen] with the contemplation of the past while observing the present."

Flag dances below sky
Squirrels scurry beneath trees
Cannon readies, facing east
JEFFREY DUBINSKY, USNA 2009

One hundred years later, although a number of new buildings have been added to the Academy grounds, Ernest Flagg's Beaux-Arts design still dominates the central Yard.

New Growth in the Twentieth Century

Increased student population in the twentieth century brought the need for more space. Luce Hall was erected in 1919 as a new building for the Department of Seamanship and Navigation. In the 1930s new buildings included the museum (Preble Hall) and the dispensary or medical clinic (Leahy Hall, called Misery Hall by the midshipmen). One of several class gift benches, the granite and limestone Class of 1897 Bench, donated by the class on their fortieth anniversary, was placed behind Tecumseh.

the cold wind blowing,
leaves scattered everywhere,
the benches empty
CHRISTOPHER MONTGOMERY, USNA 2008

In the 1950s a need for more space for physical fitness led to construction of a new field house (later named Halsey Field House) in 1956.

In 1961 Adm. Ben Moreell was appointed as head of a commission
to produce a new construction plan for the Academy. After abandoning
the first plan, which suggested annexation of historic buildings outside
the Academy gates in Annapolis, the commission contracted with John
Carl Warneke and Associates (architect of President John F. Kennedy's
gravesite in Arlington National Cemetery) to design a master plan to
accommodate the Academy's growing emphasis on technology. Over the
next few years, a complex of new structures was built: Nimitz Library,
connected by a high plaza to the new engineering facility, Rickover Hall,
and, down the steps from this plaza, the Michelson-Chauvenet math-
science complex. All of these structures were to resonate with the spirit
of Flagg's massive, gray stone structures.

The last three decades of the twentieth century brought additional
changes to the Academy, including the contemporary wooden structure
of the Robert Crown Sailing Center, with visible framework and a sharply
angled green copper roof as designed by Ellerbee and Associates of Minnesota, which was built in 1974.

A 1960s plan to replace the engineering facility and build a new auditorium was begun in 1982 with the demolition of Isherwood, Melville,
and Griffin halls and the construction of Alumni Hall, a multipurpose
space able to seat the entire brigade at one time. Lejeune Hall, built in
1982, added two new pools to the Yard. In 1992 a plan for new building
at the Academy reemphasizing water views led to a pedestrian-friendly
promenade along the water, with seating provided at the Compass Rose
Plaza and other locales. The glass walls of the Armel-Leftwich Visitor
Center, built in 1995, provide views of Annapolis Harbor.

The Twenty-First Century Academy

The terrorist attacks of September 11, 2001, at the dawn of the twenty-first century presented the United States, and the Naval Academy, with new security issues. Gate 1 near the Visitor Center was reconfigured as the main gate into the Academy. The Uriah P. Levy Center and Jewish Chapel, dedicated in 2005, provides not only separate worship space for Jewish midshipmen but also facilities for leadership and ethics training for all midshipmen.

The Glenn Warner Soccer Facility and the Max Bishop (Baseball) Stadium, along with the FitzGerald Clubhouse, provide additional facilities for soccer and baseball training; and the Wesley Brown Field House, opened in 2008, adds a new emphasis on readiness training. The Master Plan for 2014 envisions further buildings as well as new uses for older structures and expansion across the Severn River on government property, where a new ice hockey/indoor tennis facility has opened. But the National Historic Landmark status of the central Yard will ensure that Flagg's Beaux-Arts design will not be lost in "progression's march."

Professor Arbuthnot has taught in the English Department at the Naval Academy since 1981.

5 "The Changing Naval Academy: A Retrospect of Twenty-five Years"

Professor Carroll Storrs Alden

U.S. Naval Institute *Proceedings*
(June 1929): 495–501

MANY GRADUATES ARE troubled as they hear that the old Academy has undergone some modifications. In this they are not unlike their college brothers. It is hard for those long absent to believe that changes will not result in a loss of character and individuality. Yet compare the Navy of today with that of twenty-five years ago. How few of the ships of 1904, even with changed names, still remain in commission. And who would think it wisdom to hold to the same ships, the same equipment, and the same personnel—so far as this is possible? Even the colleges that are preparing the youth, not for any particular profession, but for life, by giving them a strong foundation of culture, have vastly changed. Greek has gone by the board, and there is much greater attention to the social sciences and to modern history. How could the Naval Academy, in the light of recent developments in the Navy, which is preparing midshipmen for duty on ships in which electricity now plays such a part, preparing midshipmen for assignments either related or entirely devoted to aviation, do aught else than change to meet the need? How, furthermore, could the Naval Academy, if since the World War it has caught a somewhat broader vision of the mission of the Navy, remain unconcerned as if it had no responsibility?

It happens that on June 30 I shall have completed twenty-five years of continuous service at the Naval Academy. Professors do not have silver anniversaries, but every veteran—even though his campaigns have been limited to the classroom with its struggles against the ignorance and hard-headedness of youth—enjoys looking back and reflecting.

Old and New Buildings

Mahan in his *From Sail to Steam* rejoices in the fact that his acquaintance with the Navy began with the sailing sloops and frigates, such as upheld the American honor in the War of 1812, and progressed into the marvelous steam cruisers and battleships that won the Spanish War. With a keen interest in naval tradition I have had reason similarly to be grateful that much of the old Academy was still in existence when I took my examination to qualify as an instructor on June 7, 1904. I have been a part, even though a very small part, of both the old and the new. Fort Severn, with its walls seven feet thick, built in 1809 to guard the capital of Maryland and a seaport which was then of no small consequence, stood as firmly as the day it was completed, and served as the Academy gymnasium. "Main Quarters" with the Hospital, dating from Admiral Porter's time, still occupied its position to the east or northeast of the present Officers' Club. All of the Brigade of Midshipmen, as it was then known, messed there; but in the fall of 1904 the Second Battalion (there were only two) on returning from leave was moved to the northeast wing of Bancroft Hall. As the Academic Group had not yet been begun, English, like Mathematics and Modern Languages, had its recitations in Annex C, a long frame structure that ran parallel to Chauvenet Walk, its rear looking out upon the river. Dahlgren Hall, Isherwood Hall, and the Officers' Club were completed and in use. The old Armory standing on the site of the present reservoir was to serve for several years as the chapel. The present Chapel had been begun and during the first year of its construction presented the curious spectacle of a building that was being built from the top down: that is, the great concrete dome, weighing

3,000 tons (the outer dome of terra cotta is a mere shell separated by a wide air space), was erected on eight exceedingly tall shafts of ferro-concrete, six by two and one-half feet in cross section, which carried the entire weight. It was not until the concrete dome was finished that the work of raising the light brick walls and the inner plaster walls began.

Before the Chapel was completed, General Horace Porter had discovered the body of John Paul Jones in Paris, and the hero who had been denied the expense of a funeral by the American minister in 1792 was given fitting honors when his remains were identified 113 years later. They were brought to America by a special squadron and on being received at the Naval Academy with appropriate ceremonies were placed in a small brick mausoleum, built for the purpose, between the Administration Building and Lovers' Lane. In April, 1906, the formal exercises connected with Jones were held, and President Roosevelt, Ambassador Jusserand, General Porter, and Governor Warfield were the speakers. Then the casket was moved to Bancroft Hall, being placed under the stairway leading to Memorial Hall. But John Paul Jones, adventurous to the end, would not rest until he was provided with a suitable resting place, which was found in the Crypt of the Chapel when Congress appropriated $75,000 for the purpose.

One by one the old buildings were demolished as the new were available. Even old Fort Severn in 1909 was razed to the ground, preparations being made so quietly and the work done so quickly that when outraged protesters of the Daughters of the American Revolution and other patriotic societies arrived on the scene they found nothing more than foundations to plead for. Still there was the old frigate *Santee*, the station ship where many a midshipman offender of ancient times experienced his thirty or sixty days of sea service, and where the officer in charge of the ships and his family resided. She was made the subject of poetry and romance by her adventurous crew, but few or none had reason for feeling so tenderly as I—that, however, is another story. In 1912, having been pronounced insanitary, she was ordered to be vacated by both midshipmen and the officer's family, and on one April morning of that year she was discovered to be resting on bottom, sunk at her moorings, the tide gurgling through her half open ports.

Thus the yard has come to have the appearance which we find today, when the only survivors of the old Academy consist of the two guardhouses that flank either side of the Maryland Avenue entrance. Here the candidate reporting to be sworn in may well pause, for in many a case he has caught up with his father. Here the sire paused, looking at the same bricks, the same river, half hidden but glittering through the trees, and had the same triumphant feeling as, head high in the air, shoulders thrown back, he entered upon his naval career.

Increased Number of Midshipmen

An emergency was recognized as existing after the Spanish-American War, when, in consequence of the many new ships, the officer personnel was insufficient. To meet this, Congress passed in March, 1903, a bill doubling the number of appointments, allowing for each senator and representative not one but two midshipmen. This provision was to continue for ten years. As a result the enrollment of the Naval Academy, which in 1902–03 was 393, had grown in 1904–05 to 823. This was bound to bring changes in organization and methods of instruction. Many of the officers, however, were perturbed, as indicated by a remark of a colleague of mine, Lieutenant "Pete" Russell: "Really, what can one do with this huge plebe class of 297 midshipmen? Fourteen in a section is an impossible number. Eight is the proper size, and with such one could hope to do something." If he had lived to see five midshipmen allowed for each senator and congressman in the World War, and the plebe class that in 1918 flooded into the Academy, numbering 963, he might have had added cause for reflection. Six hundred has been the approximate size of the plebe class during the last two years, and this has given ambitious instructors perhaps quite enough to work with.

Changes in Curriculum

All candidates who applied for admission to the Academy twenty-five years ago were examined in (1) punctuation and capitals, (2) spelling, (3) grammar, (4) geography, (5) United States history, (6) world's history, (7) arithmetic, (8) algebra, and (9) geometry. Since five or six of these subjects are among those usually taught in the lower schools, the youth who had left them so far behind as to be graduating from high school, or to be finishing his first or second year in college, was far from being ready to take the examination. A large number of special preparatory schools made it their business to cram for examinations and the more experienced masters reaped a golden harvest. This continued until 1920, when admission by certificate in lieu of examination was granted to those who were graduates of approved high schools or students in college, provided that their courses conformed with certain requirements laid down. In 1923 the regular examination, which still was given for those who could not qualify by certificate, was changed to correspond to the general requirements outlined by the College Entrance Examination Board. The elementary subjects were dropped and the subjects prescribed were very nearly what they are today: namely, English composition and literature, United States history, ancient history, algebra, geometry, and physics. The one further change came in 1925 when those entering by certificate were required to present not only a sufficient number of acceptable credits but also to pass what was known as a "substantiating examination"—a general examination in mathematics (algebra and geometry) and in English (composition and literature). On the introduction of the system of admission by certificate some Academy graduates were fearful that the institution would suffer from a lowering of standards. But inasmuch as the number of candidates passing the substantiating examination has run at times as low as 32 per cent their anxiety has been allayed.

In 1912 the old-time six-years' course of the midshipman, the last two years at sea, was reduced to four years, the diploma being followed immediately by a commission. This was a change not so much in study or training as in rank. Since it advanced by two years the time when the graduate might marry he regarded it as highly important.

"Semi-ans" and "ans" were abolished in 1923, and with the week in the term that had been devoted to each went the month of review, commonly dull and rather mechanical. The course in each branch was considerably extended, monthly examinations became more incisive, and in spite of the assistance of frequent short reviews the casualty lists were long enough to satisfy even the most relentless.

Naval education in general has gone forward by leaps and bounds during the period we are considering; probably the greatest gain has consisted in the establishment of the Postgraduate School at the Naval Academy and the special schools such as the Submarine School at New London and the Aviation School at Pensacola. Every young officer has the opportunity to continue his study after graduation, and comparatively few can avoid it. In the Academy itself the most marked changes are due to the introduction of courses for the study of electricity, including radio, and of aeronautics. Thus the Department of Physics and Chemistry has become Electrical Engineering and Physics; Seamanship is Seamanship and Flight Tactics; and Marine Engineering and Naval Construction is now Engineering and Aeronautics. The Departments of Mathematics and Mechanics have become fused under the name of the former. The Department of English and Law, on transferring international law and military law to Seamanship, became the Department of English, which name it still retains, although fully half of its courses are in history. Since my activities have been particularly concerned with this department I trust I shall be pardoned if I dwell with some detail on the changes it has undergone.

In 1904 the study of English was largely the study of spelling, grammar, and rhetoric. To promote the cause of accurate spelling, each midshipman at the end of the week was supposed to turn in an official report recording his delinquencies, like the following:

SIR:

I respectfully state that, during the week ending October 4, I misspelled the following words:

don't, October 1.

too, October 1.

often, October 2.

despair, October 3.

Respectfully submitted, ...

Sometimes the careless speller was still careless, and failing to consult his dictionary, misspelled a word also in his spelling report. Then he was ordered to turn in a special spelling report which read like the following:

SIR:

I respectfully state that, in my report of misspelled words dated the fifth instant, I misspelled the word written ten times herein, as follows:

despair despair despair

despair despair despair

despair despair

despair despair

Respectfully submitted, ...

In the study of grammar and rhetoric the class labored through three textbooks of rhetoric and two books of exercises dealing with words and sentences. A unique feature of the course was "Craig's Rules for the Use of Shall and Will," formulated by the head of the department two decades earlier and printed on a slip which was to be pasted in the textbook. It was not the application but the memorizing of the rules that apparently was deemed all important, and the midshipman looking for "dope" soon discovered that "Craig's Rules" were certain to appear in the monthly and also the semiannual examinations. There was an occasional short theme, but with no reading or study of literature it was a dull course.

In the study of naval history the course was limited to the achievements of the American Navy, and, in order to avoid the Sampson-Schley controversy, was stopped short of the Spanish-American War. Thus midshipmen graduated knowing nothing of Drake, Blake, Rodney, Suffren, Jervis, Nelson, Tegethoff, and Dewey. When naval history came to an end at the middle of the third-class year, the second term was devoted to English literature, one hour a week. There were fifteen exercises to cover the field, and as many of the assignments were on the lives of the authors, there was only a momentary glimpse of literature. It is so easy, however, for a later age to criticize. I wonder what the new generation will say of us.

The raising of the standard of entrance requirements has been a life-saver to the Department of English. When the changes of 1920–23 were effected we could presuppose on the part of the fourth-classman at least three years' study of English in the high schools, and many of them had had more. Accordingly we could give advanced work in composition and after two or three months change to a survey course in English literature. This begins with Malory, Spenser, and Bacon, includes three plays of Shakespeare, and does not end until we are reading the English and American authors of the present day. Naval history has been broadened so that it is a study of the sea power of all the principal nations and the influence of sea power upon history. This is followed by a substantial course in the political and social history of the United States. In the second term of the first-class year the climax is reached, so far as this department is concerned, when midshipmen are studying modern European history, beginning with 1789 and carrying it on till they are discussing the conditions and problems following the World War. Friday evenings are given to the department for public lectures, and the interest of the midshipmen is stimulated and broadened by listening to such speakers as the following (the schedule of 1929): Professor Edward

Raymond Turner, Johns Hopkins; Provost Charles Seymour, Yale; Professor James T. Shotwell, Columbia; Dr. Leo S. Rowe, Pan-American Union; Lieutenant Commander C. E. Rosendahl, U.S.N., commanding U.S.S. Los Angeles; Professor Stringfellow Barr, University of Virginia; Dr. Edmund Walsh, Georgetown; Professor William E. Lingelbach, University of Pennsylvania; Professor George H. Blakeslee, Clark University; Rear Admiral Gordon Campbell, R.N.; and the Hon. Nelson T. Johnson, Assistant Secretary of State. Such a group of lecturers would be a source of pride to any institution.

Changes in Midshipman Life

Even in 1905 midshipmen were lamenting, as recorded in the *Lucky Bag* of that year, that old customs were disappearing: "Unofficial distinctions between classes have practically vanished. Class unity and class spirit are becoming more and more difficult of attainment." It was inevitable that some of the old must go when the enrollment was doubled or trebled, and also when this increased number was in turn trebled. Yet still the Academy goes on. There must be something of great vitality in the spirit that has weathered such extremes. Let me recount a few of the changes.

Affairs of honor or sharp misunderstandings have ceased to be settled by fights. In the old days an empty room in quarters served for the ring, and an upper-classman for the referee. The difference would be settled by light-weight gloves, and discolored eyes and bruised faces later revealed how strenuous had been the effort to reach a lasting peace. Often the combatants for two or three days would be turned in at sick bay before they returned to duty, the flimsy excuse of a fall being accepted by the understanding doctors. These sanguinary contests ended in 1905 when much publicity and a serious court-martial followed a fight between a second-classman and a youngster. It went to nine or ten rounds, as I remember the story, without any real decision. At its conclusion the second-classman took a warm bath and turning in, went to sleep, a sleep from which he never roused.

Fights have ended, but boxing and almost every kind of intercollegiate sport have increased and flourished. In the old days the football team went to Philadelphia to play the Army, and the baseball team went alternate years to West Point. Otherwise, all contests were commonly on home grounds or waters, in contrast with the present plan of allowing basketball, boxing, swimming, water polo, lacrosse and every important athletic team to play at least one of their games away. Not of least importance in the education of midshipmen is the contact thus afforded with the students of colleges and the glimpses of their grounds and buildings.

The picturesque custom of baptizing the class rings of the incoming first class came to an end five years ago. It chanced that the Class of 1925, who were the performers, was large and the water in the corner of Dewey Basin near the boat shed was crowded to the limit with the hundreds diving in at almost the same instant. A catboat on which many had climbed went down, and one midshipman was soon discovered by his classmates to be in need of assistance. Resuscitation proved ineffectual. In fact the doctors surmised that death had come from heart trouble. Forthwith the ceremony of putting on class rings became a private affair.

Many were the midshipmen of earlier days who studied the "tendencies" in their rooms and had the exhilaration of a smoke without detection, which was a double exhilaration. And almost equally many, sooner or later, were caught and given a heavy assignment of demerits. This little game proved of unfailing interest. It ended when Admiral Wilson became superintendent and all midshipmen were given the smoking privilege.

Christmas leave brought the biggest change. In my first experience as an instructor recitations continued up to 3:30 p.m. Christmas Eve, and the regular study period was observed (supposedly) Christmas night. I could form some idea of the latter for we had a written exercise in naval history at eight o'clock the next morning. The same program followed New Year's Day and the morning after. During the week between, though drills were omitted, recitations continued. But let no plebe of today imagine that Academy and town in the old time knew nothing but gloom. Every midshipman had his Christmas box filled with goodies from home, and never was there such feasting for a week as in quarters. The "rag" formation Christmas morning, when the plebes might safely take unusual liberties, and when brilliant and most unexpected costumes were donned as the first class went about in early hours, supported by the band, to sing their songs, was an occasion of great hilarity. If midshipmen could not go away, every one came to them, mothers, sisters, and other people's sisters, until hotels and boarding houses in little Annapolis were crowded to the last degree and proprietors were in danger of becoming wealthy. Admiral Scales was the superintendent who changed it all by granting four days' Christmas leave. This meant the passing of many old-time customs, but no one protested except the boarding-house keepers. Admiral Wilson was a worse offender, for he increased the leave to ten days, and Christmas became the quietest season of the whole year in the yard. What has been the net result? There is the loss of many study days, not only during leave but after, for midshipmen on their return are dull and sleepy and require time before they again become normal. But the interruption is worthwhile; it relieves ennui, and the year does not seem quite so unending. I know there is a possibility that some of the commanders and lieutenant commanders may not agree with me in this and in what I am about to say further; nevertheless, I do not hesitate in affirming the belief that the Academy is a happier place today than it was in their day. There are fewer chronic "rhinos." There is not so much "frenching." One does not hear so often of the "prison walls" and the "chain gang." Of course, as all know, such words are not to be taken too seriously, but it was unfortunate that the joke should often persist after graduation with the young officers of the rank of ensign or junior lieutenant, who not infrequently would utter a prayer that they might never return to the academy for duty.

Conservative Tendencies

Classes come and classes go but their language continues much the same. This was brought to my attention when writing the biography of Commodore George Hamilton Perkins, who came to distinction as a young officer serving under Farragut at New Orleans and Mobile Bay. In home letters, written during midshipman days, he announced early in the winter of 1853 that he knew he was going to "bilge"; and when the "semi-ans" were held he added that everyone had remarked that they were "stiffer than ever before." Today, seventy-six years later, midshipmen scholastically bankrupt have the same worry, expressing it in the same language, and occasionally one, like Perkins, is turned back a year so that he may have another chance. In the *Lucky Bag* of 1905 a glossary of unfamiliar terms is included and a single glance is sufficient to disclose how much fathers and sons are alike in their speech (definitions are unnecessary for readers of the PROCEEDINGS): "bat," "bone," "brace," "bust," "canned Willie," "Christmas tree," "date," "dewberry," "drag," "frap the pap," "goldbrick," "grease," etc.

In this luxury-loving age midshipmen have maintained their simplicity to a degree that would be the envy and despair of many a college dean if he spoke his mind. In the early years of the period discussed the pay was $500 a year; today it is $780. No one would think of the added 56 per cent as leading to extravagance when the increased cost of outfit, textbooks, uniforms, and everything else is considered. No midshipman has an automobile or motor boat in Annapolis, and without special permission he does not ride in one belonging to others. Years ago an occasional upper-classman had his own canoe, in which he would appear on fine spring afternoons, especially when there was a boat race to watch. But he has not this privilege today. During leave or at graduation he may drive his own fifty-dollar bargain or his father's $2,000 sedan, but during the regular academic year Spartan simplicity still prevails.

Many of the colleges have been troubled because of the wave of liberalism (or the approach to bestiality) and the corresponding decline

of religious observance. Even "good old Yale," the bulwark of Congrega-
tionalism, after years of weighing the problem, has changed from compulsory to voluntary attendance at chapel, and the distance her students
travel on Saturday and Sunday is limited only by the car, the gasoline,
and the desire. Midshipmen report, even on a holiday, at each meal formation and on Sunday morning all go to chapel or to church in Annapolis. A few years ago one announced himself a Mussulman by conviction,
as I recall the story, and requested that he be excused from attending any
other service. The punishment fitted the crime; he was told he would
have to read the Koran and demonstrate the thoroughness of his devotion by writing a long religious essay.

The Naval Academy has had two remarkable chaplains during my
time, Chaplain Henry H. Clark, who served at this station altogether
for nineteen years, and Chaplain Sydney K. Evans, who this spring has
completed his twelfth year. Both have been a strong influence because
they have made of religion something so cheerful, manly, natural, and
far-reaching. It has been something externally healthy, and inwardly
closely linked with a man's highest impulses and feeling for service. No
matter what a midshipman's church was before he came to the chapel, he
knew he would be welcome if he joined in worship. An unusual sight in a
confirmation class was afforded a few years ago when a superintendent,
his wife, and a captain who was head of a department, with other officers
and midshipmen, went forward for confirmation. The most impressive
celebration of the Holy Communion I have ever witnessed at any institution was that at the Naval Academy at seven o'clock, Easter morning,
1927. Seven hundred communicants, six hundred of them midshipmen,
went forward to the altar rail. And the service of Easter morning of 1928
and of 1929 was each marked by a similar response. In 1927 the graduating class unanimously agreed that they would like to leave behind
them something by which the class might be remembered, and presented
the beautiful Tiffany window in the Chapel, north of the altar, entitled
"The Commission Invisible." That a class on their twenty-fifth or fifti-
eth anniversary should make such a gift might be understood, but that,

when diplomas were just in sight they should express such a warmth of feeling marked a new advance.

Twenty-five years have brought extensive changes at the Naval Academy. The old buildings have given way to new. Several officers who were midshipmen a quarter of a century ago, now as captains or commanders, have returned for duty as heads of departments. One who was a lieutenant or lieutenant commander about this time in the Department of Ordnance and Gunnery has lately been made admiral and is the commander in chief of the Battle Fleet. I wonder if officers are not more happy at being ordered to duty at the Naval Academy than they were some years ago. I feel certain that the staff of civilian professors has become much more truly a part of the Academy, and that several by their enthusiastic contribution to its life have shown that the class room is by no means the limit of their ideas and interest.

With the broadening influences that have come from the establishment at the Naval Academy of the Postgraduate School, the Experimental Station, the High-Power Radio Station, and the Naval Hospital, together with the extension of the courses in electricity, aeronautics, ordnance, English literature, and history, there has come a great increase of officers, professors, and midshipmen. The change has been almost like the merging of the small college into the university. Yet the midshipmen are still the nucleus. And in spite of the inevitable loss of much that made their life so attractive when everyone knew everyone else and when they could hold so generally to the picturesque customs of the previous half century, still the regiment of midshipmen can be safely relied on for a wholehearted devotion to the Naval Academy and to the old traditions. It is not too much to affirm that they have won nation-wide recognition for a superior manliness and power such as they have never had before.

Professor Carroll Storrs Alden was the Head of the Department of English at the Naval Academy at the time of this writing.

"The Perpetuation of
6 History and Tradition at
the Century-Old United
States Naval Academy"

Ruby Duval

U.S. Naval Institute *Proceedings*
(April 1946): 139–45

ON OCTOBER 10, 1845, the United States Naval Academy was formally opened at the historic city of Annapolis on the south shore of the Severn River, not far distant from the seat of Government in Washington. The School, as the Academy was then designated, was established on the site of an old army post, Fort Severn, which had been transferred to the Navy Department just two months earlier.

All of the original buildings, which filled the requirements of the army post and which were adequate for the immediate needs of the Naval School in 1845, have during the succeeding years been replaced by improved and larger structures. As the years passed, more land was acquired and the Naval Academy expanded its confines.

While all who were closely associated with the lives of midshipmen and officers of the old Navy and the old Naval School have long since passed away, history and tradition still survive. Historical associations and naval traditions are perpetuated for future generations by the names bestowed on the buildings of architectural beauty and the well-kept grounds with which no other naval school can compare. Thus environment plays an important role in training. The atmosphere seems to breathe of the great heroes of our Navy—heroes of the days long before this school was founded, heroes of ensuing years, and heroes of today. The buildings, the grounds, the walks, the roads, the mooring basins and the athletic fields have been given the names of great men who served our Navy and our Country well; and along the walls of the Chapel, Memorial Hall, and the Armory, memorials have been placed in honor of those graduates who have given their lives in the performance of duty.

The midshipmen's dormitory, Bancroft Hall, honors the memory of George Bancroft, the historian and diplomat, who bore an important role in the nomination of James K. Polk for the presidency in 1844. He was appointed to Polk's cabinet as Secretary of the Navy; and, recognizing a long-felt national need, he made his office especially memorable by establishing the Naval Academy as a permanent school for the education and training of midshipmen. The name of the Academy's first Superintendent, Commander Franklin Buchanan of Maryland, is recalled by Buchanan Road. Receiving his midshipman's warrant in 1815, at the age of fifteen, Buchanan soon won recognition for ability in his profession. He submitted a plan for organizing the new Naval School in 1845 in compliance with Secretary Bancroft's request, and was appointed Superintendent. Two years later he was given duty afloat and in 1852 he had command of the frigate *Susquehanna*, flagship of Commodore Matthew C. Perry in the expedition to Japan. He resigned from the United States Navy in 1861 and cast his lot with the Confederate States; he received command of the Chesapeake Bay Squadron with his flag on the reconstructed *Merrimac*; and by 1864 he had become the ranking officer of the Confederate States Navy.

The crypt below the floor of the Chapel was especially constructed to serve as the final resting place for the remains of John Paul Jones, after his body had been located in a cemetery in Paris in 1905. A Scotchman by birth, Jones came to America aboard a merchantship at an early age and won a commission as a lieutenant in the Continental Navy in 1775. He was given command of the *Ranger* in 1777 and made a memorable cruise, but his crowning success in the American Navy came in September 1779 aboard the *Bonhomme Richard* in the famous engagement with the British frigate *Serapis*.

Stephen Decatur, a young Maryland officer who won distinction in the old Navy, is honored by Decatur Road. His achievements during the Tripolitan War won for him the rank of captain at the age of twenty-five. He commanded the frigate *United States* in the War of 1812 and captured the British frigate *Macedonian*. His untimely death came in 1820 at Bladensburg, Maryland, when he was the victim of a duel with Commodore James Barron.

The name of Captain James Lawrence, who entered the Navy as a midshipman in 1797, is borne by the large athletic field in close proximity to the Postgraduate School. Lawrence saw service with Decatur in the Mediterranean during the Tripolitan disturbances and he was in command of the frigate *Chesapeake* in her action with the British frigate *Shannon* in June, 1813. His immortal words "Don't give up the ship!" uttered when he fell mortally wounded in the thick of the fight, were adopted by Commodore Oliver Hazard Perry as the slogan of his battle flag on the *Lawrence* (named for Captain Lawrence) in the Battle of Lake Erie in September of that year. This flag has been preserved and it is now conspicuously displayed in Bancroft Hall. Perry Circle honors the name of the famous fighting commodore.

The gymnasium is designated as Macdonough Hall in compliment to Captain Thomas Macdonough who entered the Navy as a midshipman in 1800. He served in the war with Tripoli, first on the *Constellation* and later on the *Philadelphia*; and in the War of 1812 he was given command of the fleet on Lake Champlain. His victory at the Battle of Plattsburg promptly brought him national distinction.

Commander George P. Upshur, the second Superintendent of the Naval Academy, has been memorialized by Upshur Road. A native of Virginia, he entered the Navy as a midshipman in 1818. He was given command of the brig *Truxtun* on her first cruise to the Mediterranean in 1843 and four years later he came to the Naval Academy as Superintendent. It was during his administration that the first addition to the original site of the former Army post was made, Congress having appropriated funds for the purchase of some adjoining property.

The beautifully parked walk which extends from the main entrance of the midshipmen's dormitory to the entrance of the Library, and over which the future admirals of our Navy march briskly to and from their classes, has been designated as Stribling Walk in memory of Commodore Cornelius K. Stribling who succeeded Commander Upshur as Superintendent in 1850. Born in South Carolina in 1796, Stribling entered the Navy as a midshipman at the age of sixteen and received his commission as a lieutenant six years later.

Goldsborough Walk bears the name of the fourth Superintendent, Commander Louis M. Goldsborough, a member of the well-known Maryland family of that name. He received his warrant as a midshipman in 1812 when but seven years of age but he saw no actual service until 1816. He had duty with the Mediterranean Squadron as a young officer and in 1830 he was put in charge of the newly established Depot of Charts and Instruments at Washington. Service afloat claimed his attention during the Mexican War and in 1853 he came to the Naval Academy as Superintendent. It was during his administration, in 1854, that the first Graduating Exercises were held at the Academy.

The fifth Superintendent, Commodore George Smith Blake, is remembered by Blake Road, on which the Administration Building, the Chapel, and the Superintendent's House are located. A native of Massachusetts, he entered the Navy as a midshipman in 1818. His duty as Superintendent extended over a period of eight years (1857–65)—the longest continuous duty for any Superintendent in the history of the Academy. It was during his administration that the Academy was removed from Annapolis to Newport, Rhode Island, during the War between the States; and with the termination of the conflict he returned the School to the city of its birth. The Navy Department's appreciation of Commodore Blake's services during this critical period was expressed in a letter addressed to him by Secretary of the Navy Gideon Welles in August, 1865.

Chauvenet Walk was named for Professor William Chauvenet, the astronomer and mathematician, a member of the Naval Academy's first staff of instructors. He served at the school for a period of fourteen years and his efforts were real contributions in formulating the courses of instruction in mathematics and navigation which were adopted for the midshipmen of his day.

Admiral David Dixon Porter, the Academy's sixth Superintendent, is recalled by Porter Road. A member of the well-known Porter family, so closely allied with the history of our Navy, he received his midshipman's warrant in 1829 and had his early training aboard the frigate *Constellation*. His father, David Porter, as a midshipman in 1799, was aboard the *Constellation* when she captured the French frigate *Insurgente*. During the Mexican War David Dixon Porter saw active service on the *Spitfire*, a small side-wheeler, and his experiences doubtless prepared him for the great conflict of 1861 in which he was destined to play an important role as commander of the sloop-of-war *Powhatan*. He distinguished himself in the capture of New Orleans and was eventually given command of all naval forces on the western rivers above that city. At the termination of the Civil War he was appointed Superintendent of the Naval Academy and his tour of duty (1865–69) has been appropriately termed "an epoch-making administration." He succeeded in securing increased appropriations for the expansion of the reservation and for the erection of adequate buildings, and he was influential in improving and broadening the course of instruction. He fostered the organization of extracurricular activities for recreation and diversion and won the respect and admiration of officers and midshipmen alike.

One of the large parade grounds, Worden Field, bears the name of Commodore John L. Worden, who was in command of the *Monitor* in her famous engagement with the *Merrimac* in March, 1862. He commanded the *Montauk* the following year and succeeded in destroying the Confederate cruiser *Nashville* which had been attempting to slip through the blockade with a cargo of cotton. He was selected to serve as Superintendent of the Naval Academy in 1869.

Rear Admiral Christopher R. P. Rodgers, who came to the Academy as Superintendent in 1874, is recalled by Rodgers Road. He was a descendant of John Rodgers of Maryland who, as a young lieutenant, won distinction on the *Constellation* in 1799. He entered the Navy as a midshipman in 1833, saw active service during the Seminole and Mexican Wars, and in 1861 he had reached the rank of commander. He served as fleet-captain aboard the *Wabash* of Admiral Du Pont's squadron at the Battle of Port Royal, and aboard the *New Ironsides* during the battle of Charleston in April, 1863. He always cherished high ideals and his administration at the Naval Academy was marked by his attempt to institute a number of reforms. He had the distinction of returning to the Academy for a second tour of duty as Superintendent in June, 1881. This was of short duration, however, as it necessarily terminated when he reached the retirement age in the early fall.

Parker Road honors the memory of Commodore Foxhall A. Parker who filled the position of Superintendent for but one short year, July 1878 to June 1879. He was the son of Foxhall Alexander Parker of Virginia who served with distinction as a naval officer in the War of 1812. Receiving his appointment as a midshipman in 1839, young Foxhall saw service in the West Indies against the Florida Indians before attending the Naval School at Philadelphia. He was commissioned as lieutenant in 1850 and held many important commands both afloat and ashore before being called to take charge of the Academy. He was keenly interested in the science of his profession and is remembered by the older officers of the Navy as reviving practical seamanship for midshipmen and sending all hands to sea on Saturday afternoons in the *Dale*, an antiquated craft which was the only available practice ship for use at the Academy at that time. His death occurred on June 10, 1879.

The succeeding Superintendent was Rear Admiral George Beall Balch for whom Balch Road has been named. He was born in Tennessee and received his appointment as a midshipman in 1837. His first cruise was made under Captain "Mad Jack" Percival aboard the *Cyane* with the Mediterranean Squadron commanded by Commodore Isaac Hull. He was with Commodore Matthew C. Perry in the diplomatic expedition to Japan in 1853 and saw active service during the War between the States nearly ten years later. After completing his tour of duty at the Academy (1879–81) he was given command of the Pacific Fleet for a short period and was retired in January, 1883.

The first graduate of the Naval Academy to have the honor of serving as Superintendent was Rear Admiral Francis Munroe Ramsay of Washington who is recalled by Ramsay Road. He entered the Navy as a midshipman in 1850, spent one year at the Academy, and then went to sea on the practice ship *Preble*. He returned to the Academy and was graduated in June, 1856. His first tour of duty as an officer at his Alma Mater came during the administration of Admiral Porter when he served as assistant to the Commandant and as an instructor in gunnery. As Superintendent (1881–86) he took direct steps to improve the practical instruction and to enforce the discipline of the school.

The large armory, Dahlgren Hall, bears the name of Rear Admiral John Adolphus B. Dahlgren who received his midshipman's warrant in 1826 and was destined to become an ordnance expert and the inventor of the first large-caliber naval gun. He served as instructor in ordnance at the Naval Academy in 1847.

An annex to Dahlgren Hall has been named in memory of Lieutenant James Harmon Ward who was selected by Secretary Bancroft in 1845 to be Executive Officer of the Naval School (Academy) and in addition to be instructor in ordnance and gunnery.

Luce Hall, which contains the academic departments of Seamanship and Navigation, and Foreign Languages, is named in honor of Rear

Admiral Stephen Bleecker Luce who received his warrant as a midshipman at the age of fourteen. He learned the rudiments of seamanship at sea, became a student at the Naval School in 1848 and was graduated with the second class to complete the course of instruction here. As a young officer and all through his interesting career his energies were directed principally to raising the efficiency of the naval personnel. He was a prolific writer and he became a recognized authority on naval education. As Head of the Department of Seamanship in 1862–63 and as Commandant of Midshipmen in 1865–68 he was afforded ample means of observing the real needs of the service. In after years, he succeeded in bringing about the founding of the Naval War College at Newport.

Rear Admiral Alfred Thayer Mahan has been honored by having the large structure which contains the Library and Auditorium bear his name. He was graduated from the Naval Academy with the Class of 1859 and his keen interest in naval strategy and history won for him world-wide renown. His chief work, *The Influence of Sea Power upon History*, was published while he was on duty as an instructor at the Naval War College in 1890 and it exercised a mighty important influence on national and international affairs.

Maury Hall, named in compliment to Commander Matthew Fontaine Maury, contains the academic departments of Mathematics, and English, History, and Government. A native of Virginia, Maury secured a midshipman's warrant in 1825 and made three extended cruises during the following nine years. His experiences soon made him recognize the need for a naval school or even a school ship, and in a series of articles contributed to the *Southern Literary Messenger* he set forth proposals for wide improvement in the service. His suggestions won the attention of senior officers in the Navy and finally, in 1845, he saw his dream realized in the opening of the Naval School at Annapolis. Commander Maury's *Wind and Current Charts and Sailing Directions* issued while he was in charge of the Depot of Charts and Instruments at Washington brought him world-wide recognition; and the Pilot Charts of today, which are sent out monthly by the Hydrographic Office, bear a caption stating that they are founded upon his researches. He resigned from the United States Navy in 1861 and offered his services to the Confederate States Government.

Rear Admiral William Thomas Sampson, the Naval Academy's Superintendent from 1886 to 1890, is remembered by Sampson Hall which contains the academic department of Electrical Engineering. He entered the Academy from New York in 1857, was graduated at the head of his class, and when he returned for tours of duty as an instructor of midshipmen in after years he did much toward expanding the work in physics and chemistry and electrical engineering.

The Marine Engineering building, Isherwood Hall, serves as an appropriate memorial to Chief Engineer Benjamin Franklin Isherwood, mechanical engineer and naval architect who entered the newly established engineer corps of the Navy in 1844. While stationed at the Navy Department in 1852–1853, Isherwood designed the first feathering paddlewheels used in the United States Navy. He became Engineer-in-Chief of the Navy in 1861 and personally directed the design and construction of machinery necessary to expand the United States' equipment afloat, from 19 steam propelled vessels in 1861 to 600 steam vessels of all descriptions by the end of the Civil War.

An annex to this building has been most appropriately designated as Griffin Hall in memory of Rear Admiral Robert S. Griffin of Virginia who graduated with the Class of 1878. He served as Chief of the Bureau of Engineering during World War I. Another annex is Melville Hall which honors the memory of Rear Admiral George Wallace Melville who entered the Engineer Corps in 1861. Interested in polar exploration, Melville volunteered for service as Chief Engineer of the *Jeanette* in the DeLong Expedition 1879. He was appointed by President Cleveland, Chief of the Bureau of Steam Engineering in 1887 and held that assignment for sixteen and one-half years.

Rear Admiral Charles J. Badger who served as Superintendent of the Naval Academy from 1907 to 1909 is recalled by Badger Road. He entered the Academy as a Cadet Midshipman in 1869 and graduated eighth in a class of twenty-nine.

Brownson Road, along the southeast boundary of Farragut Field, has been named in honor of Rear Admiral Willard H. Brownson, who served as Commandant of Midshipmen in 1894 and as Superintendent from 1902 to 1906.

McNair Road was named for Rear Admiral Frederick Valette McNair who entered the Academy from Pennsylvania and was graduated in 1857. His record for dependability and initiative led to positions of responsibility throughout his long naval career. He served as head of the Department of Seamanship at the Naval Academy from 1871 to 1875. Three years later he returned as Commandant of Midshipmen, and in 1898 he was named as Superintendent, which office he held for two years.

The extensive parade ground on the seaward side of Bancroft Hall honors the memory of Admiral David Glasgow Farragut. This is known as Farragut Field. This famous officer received his midshipman's warrant when less than ten years of age. He saw service in the War of 1812 aboard the frigate *Essex* commanded by his foster father Commodore David Porter, he was commissioned lieutenant at the age of twenty-four, and he won distinction during the War between the States when given command of an expedition against New Orleans. His flagship, the sloop of war *Hartford*, became almost synonymous with his name after the success at New Orleans and again at Mobile Bay. In after years when the *Hartford* was used as a training ship for midshipmen, the story of her gallant skipper was soon learned by all who trod her decks.

Commodore Robert L. Phythian, who served as Superintendent from 1890 to 1894, is recalled by Phythian Road. Receiving his appointment as a midshipman from Kentucky, he was graduated in 1856. It is interesting to recall that athletics had received but little direct attention until this officer's administration. On Thanksgiving Day of 1890 the midshipmen's football team, having journeyed to the Military Academy at West Point, brought down the cadets in defeat with a score of 24 to 0. This was the first football game between the two services.

Rear Admiral Philip Henry Cooper of New York, a member of the Class of 1863, is recalled by Cooper Road. He served at the Academy, as a young officer, in the departments of Seamanship and Mathematics and had opportunity to learn something of the school's need for expansion. He was selected as Superintendent in 1894 while holding the rank of captain. The following year when the Board of Visitors made strong recommendations for extensive improvements at the Academy, Captain Cooper proved to be a staunch supporter. It is said that the most important accomplishment of his administration was the inception of the rebuilding of the old school.

Colonel Robert Means Thompson, a graduate of the Naval Academy Class of 1868, who resigned from the Navy in 1871, has been honored by having his name given the large football stadium at the southwest end of Farragut Field. Always interested in the Academy, he kept in close touch with his Alma Mater and as a strong advocate of athletics he was the organizer of the Navy Athletic Association.

Eberle Road, along the northeast side of Thompson Stadium, was named in compliment to Rear Admiral Edward W. Eberle of Texas who so successfully served as Superintendent of the Naval Academy from 1915 to 1919—through the period of expansion of World War I. He was awarded the Distinguished Service Medal at the close of the war, and he served as Chief of Naval Operations from 1923 to 1927. As a young officer he had served on the *Oregon*, making the famous cruise around Cape Horn in the Spanish-American War, and he commanded her forward turret in the Battle of Santiago.

Rear Admiral William F. Fullam, who preceded Admiral Eberle as Superintendent, is recalled by Fullam Road which extends from

Buchanan Road to Dahlgren Hall. Recognized as an authority in ordnance, Fullam was called to the Academy as Head of Department of Ordnance in 1883. His shore stations in later years included the Training Stations at Newport and at Great Lakes.

The only building at the Naval Academy to be dedicated in the presence of the officer for whom it was named is Hubbard Boat House. It was dedicated on April 19, 1930, and Rear Admiral John Hubbard, then over eighty years of age, was the honor guest of the occasion. He entered the Naval Academy as a midshipman in 1866, became interested in rowing as a recreation, and was influential in organizing the midshipman crews for interclass competitions. In 1870 he served as stroke of the varsity crew which was the first to represent the Academy as a whole in any athletic event. Their race, over a three mile course, held at Annapolis on May 28, 1870, with the Quaker City Boat Club of Philadelphia, was the first in this country in which the "sliding stroke" was used.

Sands Road was named in honor of Rear Admiral James Hoban Sands who received his appointment to the Academy from Maryland and was graduated in 1863. He saw active service with the North Atlantic Blockading Squadron during the Civil War and participated in the evacuation of Charleston and both attacks on Fort Fisher. Various assignments ashore and afloat claimed him until 1905 when he was selected to fill the office of Superintendent.

In compliment to Rear Admiral John Marshall Bowyer, the Academy's 21st Superintendent (1909–11), Bowyer Road received its name. Bowyer entered the Academy from Iowa and was graduated with the Class of 1874. During the war with Spain he served as executive officer of the *Princeton*; in 1899 he was ordered to the Philippines to assist in suppressing the insurrection there; and later he saw active duty in North China during the Boxer trouble.

Dewey Basin which served as a safe mooring place for the historic yacht *America* for many years, and which is used for the Academy's cutters, half-raters, and other small craft, bears the name of Admiral George

Dewey, the hero of Manila Bay. Born in Montpelier, Vermont, in 1837, this famous officer received his appointment as a midshipman in 1854 and stood five in a class of fifteen at the time of graduation. At the beginning of the Civil War he was commissioned a lieutenant and assigned to the frigate *Mississippi*. He took part in important engagements throughout the war, and in 1868 he was ordered to the Naval Academy where he was given immediate command of the *Constitution*, the *Santee*, and other vessels used in the instruction of midshipmen. Assignments at sea followed, and he held commands with the Asiatic Squadron and with the European Squadron during the ensuing years. His next important shore duty was at the Navy Department in Washington, and in 1898 he received the command with which he won distinction in the Spanish-American War. His promotion from Commodore to Rear Admiral came in May, 1898, and the following year, through a special act of Congress, he was made Admiral of the Navy.

Santee Road and Santee Basin, while not memorializing any of the personnel of the naval service, bring to mind the old frigate *Santee* on which many midshipmen of the old Academy began their careers afloat. Tradition says her keel was laid at the Portsmouth Navy Yard in 1820 and that she was not launched until thirty-five years after. She was used as a training ship for a number of years, and when she had outlived her usefulness in that capacity she was housed over and used as the Station Ship of the Academy. In 1912 she was replaced by the *Reina Mercedes* and left her moorings to be sold and demolished.

The Naval Academy's Postgraduate School building, Halligan Hall, bears the name of Rear Admiral John Halligan, Jr., a brilliant officer who served aboard the *Brooklyn* in the Spanish-American War. Young Halligan graduated one in the Class of 1898, he served with the United States forces in France during World War I, and he was named Engineer-in-Chief of the Navy in 1927.

The road directly in front of the Postgraduate School was named in memory of Rear Admiral Richard Wainwright, a former Superintendent whose father, Commander Richard Wainwright, commanded the historic *Hartford*, flagship of Admiral Farragut, in the Mississippi operations of 1862.

Trophies of all descriptions, monuments, memorial windows, and memorial tablets, which one encounters in the course of daily routine at the Naval Academy, serve as strong influences upon the youth in training. Each has a story all its own. It may be the polished sword of the daring John Paul Jones; it may be the ensign of the frigate *Insurgente*, captured by the U.S.S. *Constellation* in 1799; it may be the simple Herndon monument in Lovers' Lane; it may be the foremast of the U.S.S. *Maine*; it may be the sextant of the gig of the *Saginaw*; it may be the tablet erected by the Class of 1909 in memory of Ensign William D. Billingsley, the first naval aviator to meet death in the performance of duty; or it may be any one of the battle flags taken by our Navy from her enemies in World War I or World War II, displayed in the Naval Academy Museum. An atmosphere of example, of loyalty, and of duty, has been built up and continues to grow in this environment of history and tradition. The United States Naval Academy of today is an embodiment of national ideals with a proud record of one hundred years. It serves not only as a noble monument to an illustrious past but as an inspiration to "carry on" and thus perpetuate the traditions of the Naval Service.

7 "The Naval Academy in Five Wars"

Louis H. Bolander

U.S. Naval Institute *Proceedings*
(March 1945): 279–89

THE UNITED STATES NAVAL ACADEMY has furnished naval officers for service in five different wars in which our country has fought; the Mexican War, the Civil War, the War with Spain, and the two World Wars. The leaders that it has supplied to the Navy have been the equals or the superiors of any that its foes could offer. These men have paid back a thousand-fold to the country's taxpayers the entire cost of equipping and running this institution for the last century. Each war has left its mark on the Academy in some way, and each war has made the public better acquainted with the solid worth of the institution which it was financing. Not only has the Naval Academy trained officers for war leadership but between wars it has kept abreast or a little ahead of naval developments so that when the embers of the next war were kindled the nation found its Navy's officers trained and ready for the next conflict. It found the Navy's equipment as good or a little better than the equipment of its opponents.

The Mexican War

When war was declared on Mexico, May 13, 1846, the Naval Academy (known as the Naval School until 1850) had been in existence but seven months. On May 14 its Superintendent, Commander Franklin Buchanan, requested the Navy Department for orders for "immediate, active service at sea." George Bancroft, the Secretary, refused his request but softened the refusal with "Were it not for the important business in which you are at present engaged, you would be one of the first on whom the Department would call." The midshipmen under his command felt a similar urge and 56 of them applied for active service. A few of the 56 applicants were rewarded for their temerity by getting almost immediate action. On May 20, 1846, a week after the declaration of war, Acting Midshipmen W. B. Hayes, Thomas T. Houston, and John Adams were ordered to report to the U.S.S. *Dale*. These three men were the first midshipmen ever ordered into active war service from the Academy. Midshipman S. S. Bassett was ordered to the brig *Truxtun* on the 25th, Acting Midshipman John R. Hamilton on May 30 was ordered to the *Dale*, and on June 2 Midshipmen Seth L. Phelps and H. G. D. Brown were ordered to report to the Commandant of the New York Navy Yard. The rest of the applicants, however, were obliged to complete their term and take their promotion examinations for Passed Midshipmen. The Board of Examiners adjourned on July 10, 1846. Those who passed their examinations of the date of 1840 (midshipmen who had first received their appointments in the year 1840) were ordered to their homes to await further orders. Forty-seven midshipmen of this date received their commissions as Passed Midshipmen, dated July 11, 1846, and were soon ordered into active service. The midshipmen of the date of 1840 who were rejected and all of the date of 1841 were permitted to go on leave of absence until October 10. The acting midshipmen (the men who had come to the Naval School without previous sea experience) were ordered to sea. It seems probable that their sea duty was given them mainly for practical experience and lasted only until the beginning of the next academic year.

The midshipmen of the date of 1840 who were promoted to Passed Midshipmen on July 11, 1846, were really the first graduates of the Naval School, though they had studied at the institution for considerably less than a year. Owing to the war Secretary Bancroft advanced their examinations by four months, making it possible for them to get into active service that much earlier.

In October, 1846, Bancroft ordered to the School about one-third of the 1841 date, who were graduated and commissioned Passed Midshipmen on August 10, 1847. Thirty-six men were in this group, thus making 90 officers furnished by the infant Naval School to the Navy, in this, the first war in which the Navy had fought since the close of our second war with Great Britain. The second group of the 1841 date had already seen active war service. There was much grumbling among the midshipmen because they were obliged to study ashore in wartime, when they all craved the excitement and possible glory of service afloat. The Secretary indeed showed them consideration by shortening their course and sending them to sea, a precedent that has been followed by the Naval Academy in all subsequent wars. But Mr. Bancroft judged rightly that the Naval School must be maintained whether or not the country was at war. Incidentally, it seems now quite possible that this Mexican War saved the School from being snuffed out early in its existence. A strong group in Congress had opposed its establishment and were equally opposed to its continuance. But their arguments could hardly carry much weight with a war in progress and with the School steadily turning out trained officers to meet service needs. During the year 1846–47 about 56 midshipmen were in attendance. These men raised a fund for the first monument to be erected in the yard, a monument in honor of the midshipmen lost at sea or killed in action during the Mexican War. It is called the Mexican Monument to this day.

On February 2, 1847, Commander Buchanan again requested sea duty and on March 2 was ordered to the command of the sloop-of-war *Germantown*. He was detached on March 8. Lieutenant James H. Ward, the Commandant of Midshipmen, acted as Superintendent until late in March when he was succeeded by Commander George P. Upshur, the second Superintendent. Ward was detached from the School the same year and served on the frigate *Cumberland* in the Gulf of Mexico. Later he was given command of the steamer *Vixen*.

During the year 1847–48 attendance was irregular. Thirty-one sessions of the Board were convened to examine 37 midshipmen for admission. They came one at a time at intervals of a few days apart. Orders came detaching them singly or in groups of two or more. No practice ships had yet been provided and there was no way of teaching them seamanship or great gun drill afloat. The irregularities in attendance, admission, and detachment of the midshipmen created an almost impossible situation. The burden of maintaining proper classes for this constantly changing student body was almost insuperable. In spite of mounting difficulties, Commander Upshur, a gentle, patient man, endeavored to meet each situation as it arose and held the School together until after the close of the war.

The Civil War

The outbreak of the Civil War, 13 years after the close of the War with Mexico, found the Academy in a vastly improved situation. The institution was now officially designated as the United States Naval Academy. It required a four-year course of its students with practice cruises each summer. Each of its students came direct from civil life. They were not known as midshipmen but as "Acting Midshipmen on probation at the Naval Academy." This cumbersome title was, however, changed by the naval reorganization act of July 16, 1862. After that date they were appointed to the Naval Academy as midshipmen. There was a special reason for this change, related directly to the exigencies of the war. As an "Acting Midshipman" his status, if captured in a practice ship by the Confederates, was questionable. But the cartel or exchange value of a midshipman was definitely fixed, at that time, as equal to seven Army or Marine privates, or to seven ordinary seamen. By this naval reorganization act the old title of passed midshipman was abolished and the new grade of ensign was established, a grade made equal to that of a second

lieutenant in the Army or the Marine Corps. Each midshipman, after graduation and upon completion of two years' service at sea, was entitled to
receive his commission as ensign. An Act of Congress of March 7, 1912,
eliminated the two years of sea service.

The Naval Academy made a very real contribution to the service during the four years of the Civil War. On January 1, 1864, there were 317
commissioned officers in the Federal Navy, who were graduates of the
Naval Academy or of the old Naval School; 142 lieutenant commanders, 85 lieutenants, 58 ensigns, and 32 acting ensigns. And on January
1, 1865, there were 138 lieutenant commanders in the service, 113 lieutenants on the active list, 21 ensigns on the active list, 32 acting ensigns,
and 31 midshipmen who had been graduated on November 22, 1864.
(For some reason these recent graduates were not yet listed as ensigns.
It seems most likely that the *Navy Register* published on January 1 of
each year was made up before or about the time of their graduation.) On
January 1, 1865, there were 455 midshipmen at the Naval Academy. Up
to the class of 1860, 72 graduates of the Naval Academy resigned, "went
South," or were dismissed. Twenty-three graduates of classes after 1860
also "went South." The oldest graduates in the service were, of course,
the officers of the date of 1840 who had been made Passed Midshipmen
on July 11, 1846. Fourteen of this date were still living and in service
when the war broke out. Twelve of these men became lieutenant commanders on July 16, 1862, the date of the naval reorganization bill, but
none of them rose above the rank of commander before the close of the
war. The Naval Academy had been in existence only twenty years when
the war closed and could furnish no officer of flag rank or even of the
grade of captain during the war. But they did add to the fleet a body of
trained, reliable, competent junior officers who were the backbone of
the service. Two men of the date of 1840, William Nelson and Samuel P.
Carter, felt that they could serve their country more effectively in the
Army and were allowed to follow their preference. Nelson was killed by
a brother officer in 1862, but Carter rose to the grade of major general in

the Army, and returning to the Navy after the war, rose to the rank of rear admiral. No other officer in the long history of either service ever has established such a record for himself in both services.

When the year 1861 opened, the clouds of war were just over the horizon. Yet the midshipmen tried hard to carry on as though nothing were amiss in the country. On January 1, according to the Officer of the Day's Journal "A large number of midshipmen were granted leave to attend the ball on board the *Constitution*." But on January 4 it was recorded that "This day was recommended by President Buchanan as a day of fasting and prayer." On January 5, "The midshipmen of the *Constitution* gave a hop this evening. Very well attended by the ladies." It should be stated here that the famed frigate *Constitution* had been brought to the Naval Academy during the previous summer. The members of the Fourth Class were quartered on board her. The Journal recorded on January 14, "All the midshipmen from Alabama sent in their resignations this P.M." On March 19 it recorded that "Mr. J. L. Lovell (Photographist) came into the Yard and commenced preparations for taking pictures of the graduating class." These pictures taken by Mr. Lovell, together with photographs of the staff of instructors and many of the Academy's buildings, were bound into a small volume, which is now in the keeping of the Naval Academy Library.

Captain William Harwar Parker, of the United States Navy and later of the Confederate States Navy, in his book, *Recollections of a Naval Officer*, gives a graphic account of happenings at the Naval Academy during the tense winter and spring of 1861:

In the summer of 1860 I was ordered to the Naval Academy for the second time, and in September reported for duty as instructor of seamanship and naval tactics, and entered upon my duties. Captain George S. Blake was at this time Superintendent of the Academy. . . . It may well be imagined that the constant state of excitement in which we were kept was not conducive to hard study; yet so good was the discipline that everything went on as usual, and the midshipmen were kept closely to their duties. As the states seceded, the students appointed from them generally resigned with the consent of their parents; but their departures were quietly taken, and the friendships they had contracted at the school remained unimpaired. Affairs remained in this state until the bombardment of Fort Sumter, April 11–13; but after that, as war was now certain, the scholastic duties were discontinued and the place assumed more the appearance of a garrison. I resigned my commission on the 19th of April 1861, upon hearing of the secession of Virginia.

After Fort Sumter had been fired upon, the rebellion of the Southern States had become so threatening that fear was felt for the safety of the Academy. The port and city of Annapolis had certain distinct advantages as a base of operations against Washington and the arms and ammunition stored at the Academy invited attack. The old frigate *Constitution* would also have been a rich prize. Under these circumstances, every possible preparation was made for the defense of the place. But the means of defense were limited. The grounds of the Academy were commanded by neighboring heights, and the *Constitution* lay aground except at high tide. On April 15, the Superintendent, Captain Blake, notified the Navy Department that he would defend the *Constitution* if it were attacked. But in the meantime the Federal Government was taking steps to insure the safety of the frigate and of the Academy. It was realized that the port of Annapolis must be kept open for the movement of troops and supplies by water to the city and thence by rail to Washington.

The story of these tense April days has been told often and well, but it has not been told better or more concisely than by the youthful midshipmen whose duty it was to keep the Officer of the Day's Journal, young men who were on the spot at the time and knew exactly what was happening from day to day.

U.S. NAVAL ACADEMY, APRIL 21, 1861.

Day opened clear and pleasant. At an early hour the acting midshipmen were ordered to assemble at their usual places of mounting guard. At 7 o'clock A.M. the steamer *Maryland* with troops on board destined for Washington City steamed in from her anchorage of the previous night and came up alongside the *Constitution*. The midshipmen on board were moved on shore in the morning and quartered in the buildings, when the *Constitution* slipped her cables and was towed out by the steamer into the stream. "Divine, Service" was not performed owing to the extra guard mounting. After supper the drum beat to quarters for the purpose of "inspection," after which regular guard was mounted and sentinels and patrols were distributed about the Yard.

Respectfully submitted,

H. E. Mullan.

The steamer *Maryland*, mentioned by Midshipman Mullan, was a Chesapeake Bay ferryboat commandeered by General Benjamin F. Butler, and the troops on board her were the 8th Massachusetts Regiment, commanded by Butler himself.

With the *Constitution* safely at anchor in Annapolis Roads and with Butler's troops on the Academy grounds, all fears for the safety of the institution seem to have disappeared that Sunday morning of April 21. For further events let us return to the faithful Journal:

APRIL 22, 1861.

Commenced clear and pleasant with a light breeze from the Sd. and Wd. At 4.30 a.m. the steamer *Boston* with the N. Y. State Regiment on board hove in sight and stood into the harbor. At 5 p.m. the Boston came alongside the long wharf, landed her troops, which after disembarking were drawn up in the rear of the Recitation Hall and Midshipmen's Quarters. The members of the Seventh Regiment were quartered for the night in the different rooms of the Recitation Hall. There were no recitations or exercises for the Midshipmen today they being occupied throughout the day in extra guard duty. The steamer *Maryland* with Massachusetts troops on board is still aground on the shoal off Greenbury Point. The school ship *Constitution* is safely anchored in Annapolis Roads.

Respectfully submitted,

John W. Philip.

The John W. Philip who signed the above entry was the Captain "Jack" Philip of Spanish-American war fame, who admonished his men after the Battle of Santiago: "Don't cheer, boys, those poor fellows are dying."

APRIL 23, 1861.

This day commenced clear, cold and pleasant and continued so throughout. The usual calls to studies and recitations were sounded but no recitations were heard, the Recitation Hall being occupied by the troops now in the grounds. The acting midshipmen were exercised by Professor Lockwood in infantry and artillery tactics combined. During the forenoon the steamer *Maryland* was gotten off the bar and her troops to the amount of about 600 were landed.

APRIL 24, 1861.

Several steamers with troops on board hove in sight. These troops were destined for Washington. Among the vessels were the *Baltic* and the Coast Guard Steamer *Harriet Lane*. Several thousand more troops were landed and were quartered in the Yard, occupying the midshipmen's class rooms. Ten of the First Class received orders to report to Washington.

One of the ten members of the First Class so ordered was Midshipman William T. Sampson, later Superintendent of the Naval Academy and commander of the North Atlantic Squadron in our War with Spain.

As Captain Parker has already stated, most of the midshipmen from the South resigned when they received word that their native states had seceded. According to the *Navy Register* issued January 1, 1863, 152 acting midshipmen resigned between December 4, 1860, and July 1, 1862, and 13 were dismissed. It seems quite possible that many of the later resignations were for reasons other than political, but from December 4, 1860, to July 1, 1861, there were 106 resignations. Certainly the greater part of these resignations submitted at a time when political feeling in the country was at fever heat must have been made because the men wished to return and follow the fortunes of their home state. Many had postponed leaving their friends at the Academy until after Fort Sumter had been invested and war appeared certain. But on April 19, 3 midshipmen resigned; on April 20, 11 resigned; on April 23, 4; on April 24, 3; and on April 25, 12. Many dramatic scenes took place in the closing days of the Academy. Southern midshipmen said good-by to their friends from the North with tears running down their cheeks. Northern men escorted their southern companions to the Academy gates and shook hands in a last farewell. Some of these friends were to meet each other in the next four years in deadly battle. In other cases the leave-taking was final. They would never again meet.

By April 25 the routine of the Academy had been disrupted utterly. On the 24th the remaining midshipmen were transferred to the *Constitution*, still lying in Annapolis Roads. Captain Blake wrote the Department recommending the immediate removal of the Academy. He proposed Fort Adams at Newport, Rhode Island, as the most available place and suggested that the steamer *Baltic* then lying in the harbor should be used to transport the officers, civilian instructors, and their families. As there was no likely chance that instruction could be resumed at Annapolis for a long time the Department readily approved his recommendations. On

April 27 Captain Blake was officially ordered to remove to Newport. All the books, models, and apparatus that could be moved were stowed on board the *Baltic*. The officers and their families embarked on her on May 5 and on the evening of May 9 arrived in Newport. The *Constitution* under the command of Lieutenant G. W. Rodgers with the midshipmen on board left Annapolis on April 25 and on April 29 reached the New York Navy Yard. From New York they sailed for Newport arriving there on the evening of May 9 about 2 hours before the *Baltic*. Soon after May 10 the remaining members of the First Class and all the members of the Second and Third Classes, except for a few who remained to assist in discipline, were detached and ordered into active service. By May 13, just 18 days after the *Constitution* had left Annapolis, the Academy was again in full operation.

As the fort failed to provide adequate or comfortable accommodation for the officers and the upper class of midshipmen, the Atlantic House, a large hotel in the central part of the city, about ten minutes' walk from the water front, was leased by the Government for one year. This hotel, built in 1846, stood at the corner of Bellevue Avenue and Pelham Street. Its site is now occupied by the Elks' Club. On September 21 the upper class, those who had entered the Academy in the summer of 1860, were moved to this hotel, the *Constitution* being given over to incoming members of the new Fourth Class. The taking over of the hotel was done with considerable ceremony. The Battalion was marched to its new quarters preceded by the band. The ensign was hoisted above the hotel. The Battalion was then addressed by Mayor Cranston of Newport and by Captain Blake. The first recitation was held in the Atlantic House on September 23, 1861.

For the most part the days passed at the Academy as if there were no war going on but a few hundred miles away. But on November 15, 1861, a salute of 21 guns was fired from the *Constitution* in honor of Flag Officer Dupont's success in the capture of Port Royal, South Carolina, on November 7.

On December 7 a midshipman was placed under close confinement for playing at cards. Throughout the four years spent at Newport one finds numerous references in the Journal to midshipmen being punished for smoking, for playing cards, or for having cards or tobacco in their possession. In the autumn of 1862 the members of the First and Second Classes petitioned Secretary Welles for the privilege of smoking but their petition was denied. On December 23, 1862, football playing in the hotel or in the immediate vicinity was forbidden and four days later football playing was prohibited until further orders were given. Captain Blake was a splendid officer; his patriotism, zeal, and professional competence were unquestioned. But, at this day, it does seem that he erred in being too strict with the young men under his charge in what were, after all, but trivial matters. And in curtailing or forbidding athletic activities he was doing positive harm to the midshipmen and encouraging indirectly many mischievous activities that would scarcely have been thought of if these young men could have worked off their surplus energies in healthful outdoor recreation. The practice of hazing is said to have been started in 1862 while the school was under this too-puritanical regime. The testimony of a foreign observer bears out some of the above observations. On February 23–24, 1864, Captain J. G. Goodenough, of the Royal Navy, visited the Academy. His comment on the Academy in his diary is most illuminating for it depicts the school as seen through unprejudiced eyes:

NEWPORT (NAVAL ACADEMY), FEBRUARY 23RD.
This college is more advanced than our Britannica . . . If application and study are of any use, I'm afraid that these people will have very superior men to ourselves in their navy. They are working harder and more intelligently for it than we are . . . But the boys don't seem to get exercise enough. I can't make out that they have any games, or outdoor amusement either.

During the summer of 1862 cruises were made on the *Marion* and *John Adams*, keeping close watch for Confederate raiders. The commanders of these two ships, Lieutenant Commander Stephen B. Luce and Lieutenant Commander Edward Simpson, were directed to overhaul every vessel that they met and satisfy themselves as to her identity. Though every midshipman watched with great excitement the firing of blank cartridges and shots across bows, no captures were made. The summer cruise was made again in 1863 on the *Marion, Macedonian,* and yacht *America* which had recently been given to the Academy. The *Marion* was ordered to search for the Confederate raider *Tacony* which had been reported burning vessels on the New England coast. The *Macedonian* crossed the Atlantic and visited Plymouth, England.

The Naval Academy grew steadily in numbers during its sojourn in Newport. On January 1, 1861, four months before leaving Annapolis, there were 267 midshipmen in attendance; on January 1, 1862, after deducting the large number of resignations of men from the Southern States, there were 318 midshipmen at the Academy; on January 1, 1863, there were 386; on January 1, 1864, there were 457, but on January 1, 1865, because of the graduation of 2 classes in 1864, there were only 455. The first of these graduation exercises was held on June 8, 1864, the speaker on this occasion being the Hon. James A. Hamilton, of New York. The subject of his address was, "Personal and Public Characters of Naval Officers." There were 29 men in this group, all men who had entered the Academy in 1860 and had come to Newport after one year at Annapolis. On November 22, 1864, the second graduation took place for this year. There were 31 midshipmen in this group, all of the date of 1861, and all of whom had come to the Academy after it had been established at Newport. The Officer of the Day's Journal simply records: "At 11.45 beat to quarters and assembled in the Main Hall to witness the presentation of diplomas to the graduating class. Study hours were suspended until 2 P.M." No mention of a speaker at this ceremony was made in the Journal and no record of any speaker can be found. This was the last graduation ceremony to be held at Newport. The Congress, on May 21, 1864, passed an act providing that the Naval Academy should be returned to its old quarters at Annapolis before October, 1865.

On April 11, 1865, 2 days after Lee's surrender at Appomattox, a salute of 36 guns was fired "in honor of the recent great victories of the Army and Navy." In the evening a large bonfire was built in front of the Academy. Four days later news came of the assassination of President Lincoln. The flag of the Academy was lowered to half-mast. On June 22, 1865, the midshipmen left Newport for their summer cruise on the *Macedonian, Marion,* and the steam sloops *Marblehead* and *Winnipec.* These ships were to return the midshipmen to Annapolis at the end of their cruise. During the summer of 1865 the Academy equipment and the books of the Library were boxed and brought back to Annapolis. The officers, instructors, and their families were also returned to Annapolis, ready to greet the midshipmen on their return.

But what was happening in the old Naval Academy quarters at Annapolis while the school was sojourning at Newport? On October 6, 1864, a letter was written to the editor of the newly established *Army and Navy Journal,* signed "Graduate," and published in the *Army and Navy Journal* of October 22. This letter describes in considerable detail the condition of the grounds while under the control of the Army:

Can you find space in the *Journal* for a few thoughts suggested by a short visit to the Naval Academy grounds at Annapolis by one of the many who had to leave its pleasant location, because of the then doubts as to the loyalty of Maryland to the Federal Government? After its hasty evacuation by the Navy, the buildings and grounds were taken possession of by the Army as a military post; then began the work of destruction, until it was so notorious that the Navy Department was compelled to order a naval officer there, to check, if possible, the desolation of the property. After being occupied for about 16 months as a military post, it was turned over to the Medical Department of the Army as a general hospital . . . My eyes were struck by the view of a number of hospital tents occupying the grounds once held sacred from the footprints of any one. Around these tents were trodden innumerable footpaths, marring the beauty of the grounds. Next came an unsightly board fence dividing the upper from the lower grounds; then came roads and pathways, made on pavements and grass plots, the crossing of which once subjected a student to demerits . . . The fine buildings I found occupied in various ways. Most of them are used as hospitals, while other portions are given up as sutler-shops, where lager-beer, etc. is dispensed. The fine old quarters of the Superintendent are used as a billiard saloon. What a transformation from their once legitimate use. Within the enclosure is also a barber-shop, tailorshop, photograph gallery, etc. Thousands of dollars will be required to restore this valuable institution to its original condition. Meanwhile every friend of the Navy looks forward with interest to the day when the operations of the Academy may be resumed there.

This indignant letter writer, no doubt, felt justified in his criticisms. But it must be recalled that the nation was then engaged in its greatest and bloodiest war up to that time, and with streams of wounded men coming from the Southern battlefields to the hospital, there was little time to be given for the meticulous care of the grounds and buildings which the Army had temporarily under its control.

When, 33 years after Appomattox, we found ourselves at war with Spain, the Navy was an entirely different organization from that of the Civil War. Its wooden ships had for the most part been replaced by steel armored craft. Its regular officers were now practically all graduates of the Naval Academy, then rounding out its fifty-third year of service to the Republic. Every officer of flag rank, every captain, and most of the other officers had received their diplomas from Annapolis. Dewey was of the class of 1858, Schley of the class of 1860, and Sampson headed the class of 1861 and was in the first group of ten to be called into active service. By the end of June, 1897, 2,307 men had been graduated from the Naval Academy.

The Spanish-American War

On February 16, 1898, the Officer of the Day's Journal carried this ominous announcement: "Received news of the blowing up of the U.S. Battleship *Maine* in Havana Harbor with the loss of many lives." On February 26 the *Army and Navy Journal* announced in its Annapolis news-letter:

> News of the loss of the Battleship *Maine* has caused a suspension of social activities in Annapolis. On Sunday the Chapel and the Annapolis Churches made special reference to the disaster. A subscription is being made up in Annapolis for a fund for a memorial to be erected in memory of the heroes of the *Maine*.

The Navy Department decided to graduate the Class of 1898 two months ahead of schedule in order that they might be sent to sea. On April 2, 1898, this class of 39 members received their diplomas. It was a simple, brief ceremony. A short address was made by Commander Edwin White, the Commandant of Midshipmen. On May 17, 1898, the death of Ensign Worth Bagley was announced. Bagley, who was graduated with the class of 1895, was a well-known figure in the city, as he had become famous for his athletic ability. His death brought the war close to the Academy. On May 24 it was decided to abandon the summer cruise; 123 of the cadets (the official name given to midshipmen at that time) were ordered to ships actively engaged in the prosecution of the war. On July 12 a mass meeting was held in the city. At this meeting it was voted to tender to Commodore Schley, his officers and men, congratulations and thanks for the splendid victory at Santiago. Later there would be a nation-wide debate as to who should claim credit for the victory, Sampson or Schley.

Probably the most colorful event at the Naval Academy during this short war with Spain was the sojourn of the Spanish Admiral Cervera and his officers at the Academy after their capture subsequent to the destruction of the Spanish fleet at Santiago. On July 16 they reached the city and were quartered in what was then known as Buchanan Row. Admiral Cervera, who, a few short weeks before had been regarded as some sort of an ogre to be feared and dreaded, turned out to be a handsome, dignified, elderly gentleman with most charming manners. The officers who came with him proved to be charming gentlemen, too. After giving their parole not to leave the city they were allowed to go about as they pleased and were invited into the homes of officers stationed at the Academy and to the homes of the people of the city, who vied with each other in offering them every courtesy and hospitality. One middle-aged lady told this writer that she well remembered Admiral Cervera, though she was but a very small girl at the time, and that meeting her on the street he actually patted her on the head. These prisoners-of-war bicycled and took walks about the streets where they soon became well-known figures. Though technically they were prisoners-of-war, their treatment, was about as different from that usually given to such prisoners as could well be imagined. At the conclusion of hostilities they left the Naval Academy for their homes in Spain and took with them the good will of everyone. As far as is known, not one untoward incident marred their stay at the Naval Academy.

World War I

Some 20 years later, owing to the precarious situation of the world in general and the increasing threat of war with Germany, it was decided to graduate the class of 1917 two months in advance of the regular time. This class that had entered in 1913 and now consisted of 182 members was graduated on March 29, 1917, almost 19 years since the day when the class of 1898 had been graduated. The speakers at the ceremony were the Secretary of the Navy, Mr. Josephus Daniels, and the Superintendent, Captain Edward W. Eberle. There had been, with the graduation of this class, 4,823 graduates of the institution since its founding in 1845. Eleven days before, the student officers at the Postgraduate School had received orders assigning them to special duty, discontinuing the work of the school.

On April 6, 1917, the Superintendent published and posted at the evening roll call the following ominous announcement:

Sixteen ALNAV—The President has signed Act of Congress which declares that a state of war exists between the United States and Germany. . . . Acknowledge 131106. Secnav.

We had now embarked on the greatest war that had been fought thus far in world history. The Naval Academy prepared to do its part in the grim realities that lay ahead. During that spring of 1917 no athletic contests were held at the Naval Academy. Late that spring an Italian Commission with Prince Udine at its head visited the institution. In June, Prince Hiroaka Tamura, a former Naval Academy graduate, was also a visitor. The Japanese were at that time our allies. On June 28, 1917, the class that had entered in 1914 and which would normally graduate in 1918, were given their diplomas. This class was made up of 199 men. The speakers at the ceremony were again Mr. Daniels and Captain Eberle. Mr. Daniels presented the diplomas. Shortly after the outbreak of war it was decided by the Department that it would be necessary to train many more officers for service with the fleet than the Naval Academy could possibly supply by any ordinary means. Our Navy was expanding with giant strides and steps had to be taken to supply its ships and men with trained officers. On June 2, 1917, a letter was sent to Captain Eberle outlining a proposed plan for training additional officers and calling upon the Naval Academy to do its part. Captain Eberle acquiesced promptly with this plan. Young men from all parts of the country and from all walks of life were offered a short course at the Academy to fit them for service with the fleet. They must have had at least two years of college work and must, of course, meet certain rigid physical requirements. The course given them was planned to be as practical as possible with no unnecessary frills. It comprised navigation, gunnery, and seamanship for deck officers; electrical and marine engineering for engineer officers; and Navy regulations and naval customs for both branches. Before they reported at the Naval Academy they were commissioned as Ensigns in the U.S. Naval Reserve Force, though a few with special qualifications were commissioned as Lieutenants, junior grade. Young men came to the Academy from every part of the country. Many held degrees from civilian colleges and technical schools. Many had held positions in the professional or business world before aspiring to be naval officers. Others had served as enlisted men and petty officers in the U.S. Naval Reserve Force before the war. They were somewhat older than the regular midshipmen, their average age being 29. They wore, while under instruction at the Academy, khaki uniforms, in striking contrast to the blues and whites of the regular officers and midshipmen.

The first group arrived on July 5, 1917, and were detached on September 14, 1917, after two months' intensive training. On graduation, these men for the most part were given temporary commissions in the regular Navy. If they failed in not more than one course they were sent to sea but were not given temporary commissions. In the event that they showed the necessary ability they would then be given temporary regular commissions. There were 169 in this first group of Reserves. Five such groups were graduated from September 14, 1917, to January 25, 1919. The largest group, the fourth, with 523 members were graduated September 18, 1918. Several other special groups, civil engineers, pay officers, assistant naval constructors and others, were also trained at the Academy. In all the Naval Academy supplied 2,569 graduates from these groups of Reserves for the naval service.

The first Reserves to arrive were quartered in Bancroft Hall but in the summer and fall of 1917 temporary wooden barracks were erected on the tennis courts running parallel to Dewey Basin. These quarters were ready for occupancy by December, 1917. All later groups were quartered in these barracks. Each group of Reserves was divided into two battalions of two companies each. They took up sports with enthusiasm and interbattalion contests took place in baseball, tennis, and crew.

In the summer of 1917, 744 plebes were sworn in, the largest entering class in the Academy's history until then. But the next summer a still larger class of 971 members was admitted. On July 5 bids were opened for the construction of two new wings to Bancroft Hall to house the greatly enlarged group of regular midshipmen. So great was the demand for housing the midshipmen that a section of the Fourth Class were quartered in the Marine Barracks, now the quarters of the Postgraduate School. Interest in football was as great as ever and on September 5, 1917, the new coach, Mr. Gilmour Dobie, reported for duty. Memorial services were held in the Chapel October 28 for the men who had lost their lives in the naval service thus far in the war with Germany. On November 18 members of the French Commission and French Army officers were the guests of the Superintendent. In April, 1917, it was decided to graduate the Class of 1919 on June 6, 1918, decreasing the four-year course to three for the duration of the war. In April, 1918, it was ordered by the Navy Department that all midshipmen at the Academy must learn how to swim before they could be graduated. On June 6, 1918, Secretary of the Navy Daniels presented their diplomas to the graduating class of 199 members. On October 10 Sir Eric Geddes, First Lord of the Admiralty, visited the Academy as the guest of Secretary Daniels. On November 23, one of the strangest incidents in football history took place at the Academy. A game was being played between the Great Lakes Naval Training Station and the midshipmen. A Navy substitute sitting on the sidelines ran out and tackled a Great Lakes man, causing a touchdown to be conceded to Great Lakes. The midshipmen lost the game, 7–6.

Life at the Naval Academy went on about the same during the first World War as if there had been no war. The war was discussed, read about in the newspapers and magazines, officers were detached and ordered to sea and officers fresh from sea duty took their places as they had been doing for over 70 years.

World War II

In the present World War little outward differences can be noted. The guards carry pistols and are even more vigilant at the gates. Visitors cannot enter the yard without a pass. The presence of many reserve midshipmen is noticeable as well as many reserve officers though they cannot be distinguished outwardly from the regulars.

The Second World War came very suddenly to the Academy on that Sunday afternoon of December 7, 1941. When the fatal word came that the Japs were attacking Pearl Harbor, sightseers were herded out of the gates. The watchmen were armed immediately and patrol boats were sent out to guard the water front. A dance was under way in Smoke Hall when the guards swarmed in and escorted the girls out of the gates. Then the Academy settled down with grim seriousness to the business of war. It had been foreseen, of course, that war was in the making and few doubted but that we would soon be in it. So, long before the Pearl Harbor attack the Academy had begun to prepare for eventualities. Two new wings were added to Bancroft Hall, and a new classroom building, Ward Hall, named in honor of the first gunnery instructor at the old naval School, was constructed for the use of the Department of Ordnance and Gunnery. About 30 acres were added to the grounds by purchase and by reclamation from the Severn River. The minimum age limit for midshipmen was raised from 16 to 17. During the year 1941, the Academy sent out two classes of regular midshipmen. On February 7, 1941, the regular class of 1941 was graduated; and on December 19, twelve days after the Pearl Harbor attack, the regular class of 1942 received their diplomas. By increasing the midshipmen appointments allotted each Congressman from four to five, and with proportionate increases in the other categories of appointments, the Naval Academy had in October, 1941, the largest enrollment in its history, for there were over 3,100 midshipmen here at that time. It required the services of over 350 officers and civilians to instruct these men. The majority of the officers on instruction duty were and are retired officers called back to active duty or officers in the Naval Reserve.

The course was shortened by a full year, eliminating entirely the Second Class. Yet it was found possible to give about 95 per cent as much instruction in three years as had been formerly given in four. This was done, for the most part, by changing the normal summer schedule, so that about one-third of the midshipmen followed a modified academic program for the summer. This program has been followed substantially as outlined through the three war years. Since 1940, 3,257 regular midshipmen have been graduated from the Academy.

About two weeks after the outbreak of war the Superintendent, Rear Admiral Russell Willson, was ordered to Washington to serve on the staff of Admiral Ernest J. King. He was succeeded by Rear Admiral John R. Beardall, who has been retained in that position until the present time.

Early in 1941 the Academy's gates were opened to groups of young men from civilian colleges throughout the country who are known as Midshipmen of the U.S. Naval Reserve. They are given intensive courses in strictly professional subjects: marine engineering and electrical engineering. The first group, however, that was graduated on May 15, 1941, was divided into two sections: deck officers and engineers. The deck officers were given courses in seamanship and ordnance and gunnery. All subsequent groups have been engineers only and have been given engineering instruction. These Reserve Midshipmen are quartered and messed in Bancroft Hall, but have few contacts with the regulars. Their uniforms are blue, exactly like those of the regular midshipmen, except that each Reserve wears a thin band of gold braid on each cuff three inches long. In the last three and one-half years 3,319 of these Reserve

Midshipmen have been graduated from the Academy in ten different groups. Upon graduation each man is given a commission as an Ensign in the U.S. Naval Reserve.

In addition to the routine training of regular midshipmen and the intensive training of Reserve Midshipmen, in the summer of 1941 a group of graduates from technical schools from different parts of the country was brought to the Academy for a month's indoctrination course in Navy regulations and naval traditions and customs. These men were commissioned in the Naval Reserve before coming to the Academy. At the conclusion of the course they were sent out as ordnance inspectors wherever munitions for the Navy were being turned out.

These are busy days at the Academy, inspiring days, never-to-be-forgotten by the officers and civilians serving here. If George Bancroft, the Navy's Secretary, who first visited the grounds of Fort Severn in the summer of 1845, should visit them now, he would find little in this huge, modern, busy wartime institution to remind him of sleepy old Fort Severn.

A graduate of Syracuse University and the Library School of the New York Public Library, **Mr. Bolander** has been assistant librarian at the U.S. Naval Academy for twenty years. He has contributed numerous articles to the *Proceedings* and is a constant aid to the Institute in problems of research.

8 "A Hundred Years of the Naval Academy"

Louis H. Bolander

U.S. Naval Institute *Proceedings*
(April 1946): 147–52

THE NAVAL ACADEMY on October 10, 1945, celebrated the hundredth year of its existence. Due to wartime conditions the ceremonies were simple but dignified and fitting for the occasion. On May 3, President Truman approved a Congressional resolution which created a United States Naval Academy Centennial Commission, made up of 15 members including himself, charged with the responsibility of formulating plans for the celebration.

The Naval Academy, the largest and most celebrated institution of its kind in the world today, has sent its graduates to serve in the five wars in which the nation has participated since its founding. In the Mexican War 90 Passed Midshipmen served who had just left the fostering care of the fledgling Naval School. Though the Naval Academy was but 16 years old when the Civil War broke out in 1861, about 350 of its graduates served in all grades up to lieutenant commander, and a few reached the grade of commander a month before Appomattox. In the Spanish-American War, in the first World War, and in the second World War every officer of flag rank was an Academy graduate. Its graduates include world-famous names such as Dewey, Sampson, Schley, Sims,

Rodman, King, Nimitz, Halsey, Mitscher, Spruance, Hewitt, Kirk, Old-
endorf, Kinkaid, and Turner. Its graduates have explored the arctic, the
Antarctic, and the far reaches of the Pacific; they have made the Stars
and Stripes known and respected on the Seven Seas of the world.

Many of its graduates who have returned to civil life have distinguished themselves in business, industry, science, literature, and public
life. Perhaps the most famous of all its graduates in the world of literature is Winston Churchill, of the Class of 1894, author of novels like
Richard Carvel, The Crisis, Coniston, and other books depicting American life. The Academy's most famous scientist is undoubtedly A. A.
Michelson of the Class of 1873 who by meticulous experiment determined the velocity of light while he was an Ensign on duty at the Academy. Its most famous inventor is probably Frank J. Sprague of the Class
of 1878 who built the first successful trolley car in the United States.
The list of Academy graduates who have made significant contributions
to the life of the nation could be almost indefinitely prolonged if space
permitted. But the Naval Academy's greatest glory is its thousands of
graduates of whom the country rarely hears, officers who have fought our
ships on every sea, facing death in every form every minute of every day,
always mindful of the call of duty. These unsung heroes are the backbone
of our fleet.

This hundred years of the Academy's existence has been a century
of incredible change in almost every phase of human life. When the first
Superintendent gave his address to the assembled midshipmen, October
10, 1845, there was not a telephone, a radio, an airplane, an automobile,
or even a trolley car in the entire country. A man who had lived in Shakespeare's day would have felt more at home in the Annapolis of 1845 than
would an Annapolitan of 1845 in the world of today. And a seaman of
the Spanish Armada would have felt more at home on a sailing ship of
our Navy in 1845 than would an American bluejacket of 1845 in a modern destroyer. In that year our Navy possessed just 76 ships, 8 of them
steamers, not an armored ship in the lot. A single one of our modern
destroyers, let us say of the 2,100-ton Fletcher class, with its 5-inch guns,

could have blown our entire fleet of 1845 out of the water in a couple of hours, if that fleet could have been assembled within range. The displacement of just two of our *Iowa* class battleships would about equal the combined tonnage of these 76 ships. Today our fleet includes 26 of the most powerful battleships in the world, with aircraft carriers, cruisers, destroyers, and submarines to make it by far the greatest fleet in the world's history, equipped with the most intricate machinery that the brain of man can devise. It has been the business of the Academy's graduates to keep step with this world of change. In naval developments these men have kept our Navy abreast or a little ahead of the navies of our enemies real or potential, and the navies of our friends as well.

Fifty-six years elapsed between the inauguration of George Washington as our first President and the founding of the Naval Academy; and forty-eight years were to pass after the launching of the Navy's first ship before Annapolis became the seat of American naval education. In those formative years of our country's history eleven different men were inaugurated as President and three different wars were fought in which the Navy participated. This "Golden Age" of our Navy gave birth to such gallant figures as Stephen Decatur, David Porter, Thomas Truxtun, Oliver Hazard Perry, John Rodgers, and others like them. These men gave our Navy an inspiration and a tradition which has been carried on by their successors and still lives today. A Navy without such a tradition disintegrates under stress of hardship and disaster. Witness the debacle of the German Navy in 1918 and again in 1945.

This period saw many efforts made by Presidents, Secretaries of the Navy, Congressmen, naval officers, and private citizens to improve the system of education of the Navy's junior officers. The first of such proposals was made by President John Adams who transmitted to Congress on January 14, 1800, a plan drawn up by James McHenry, his Secretary of War. This plan provided for a military academy, one division of which should be called a "School of the Navy" where all future naval officers should be trained. Thomas Jefferson and John Quincy Adams also made proposals for some better system of naval education.

Improvements in the system came gradually as do most things worthwhile. The Navy regulations of 1802 instructed the ships' commanders to see that the "schoolmasters" performed their duty toward the midshipmen by "diligently and faithfully instructing them in those sciences appertaining to their department." As no schoolmasters had been provided by Congress, the 1802 regulations provided that the chaplain should perform the duties of schoolmaster. In 1813 Congress provided that every ship-of-the-line (huge sailing ships armed with 60 to 100 guns) should have a schoolmaster on board who should be charged with the education of the midshipmen assigned to that ship. By 1831 it was provided that no vessel the size of a sloop-of-war or upwards should sail without a schoolmaster on board, if one could be had, to instruct the midshipmen.

As early as 1803 a school for midshipmen was established under the direction of Chaplain Robert Thompson at the Washington Navy Yard. Here he gave courses in mathematics and navigation. Thompson continued on this duty until 1810, gradually extending the system until it embraced the New York, Philadelphia, and Norfolk Navy Yards. Midshipmen might attend these schools if they were interested. Most of them were not interested except insofar as these schools provided short courses to prepare for examinations for promotions. They wanted the exact amount of culture that would enable them to pass their examinations, and no more. This instruction on shipboard and ashore, due to the interruptions incident to naval life, was incomplete and intermittent though it did produce some outstanding naval officers.

A more ambitious scheme of education was put forward in 1839 when a school for midshipmen was established at the old Naval Asylum in Philadelphia. Midshipmen, all of whom had seen service at sea, were ordered to attend this school. And for six years this school gave regular courses of eight months each to midshipmen who were sent here to prepare for their promotion examinations for Passed Midshipmen (a grade equivalent the present Navy grade of Ensign). To this school in 1842 came a young Yale graduate only 22 years of age. This young man, William

Chauvenet, was not only a brilliant mathematician and astronomer but also a capable, gifted teacher. He drew up a plan for a two-year course for the school which was approved by the Secretary of the Navy but was rejected by his successor. To this school also came as instructors two able teachers, Lieutenant James H. Ward of the Navy, an expert in naval gunnery and in naval tactics, and Henry H. Lockwood, a graduate of West Point.

The same year that Chauvenet came to the Philadelphia School, a Corps of Engineers was established in the Navy. This was the first definite recognition by law of the important part that steam was destined to play in the fate of navies and nations in the years ahead. Perhaps no other single factor played so large a part in the final establishment of a definite system for training naval officers ashore as the introduction of steam as a propulsive power for ships. No longer could it be argued that a midshipman could acquire aboard ship all he should ever need to know to make him a competent naval officer.

Three years later, on March 11, 1845, when James K. Polk was inaugurated the eleventh President of the United States, he invited George Bancroft, a distinguished New England philosopher, historian, and diplomat, to sit in his cabinet as his Secretary of the Navy. On May 1, seven weeks after his appointment, he addressed duplicate letters to four instructors at the Philadelphia Naval School regarding the nature of their duties. Since it is his first letter in the archives of the Navy Department on the subject of naval education it seems worth quoting verbatim here:

> Sir, I request that you will report to me the nature of the duties performed by you at the Naval School during the last year, the number of hours you have been employed daily, the number of students employed by you during that period, and also offer any suggestions for the improvement of the school which may seem to you advisable.
>
> I am respy Your Obdt. Servant
> GEO. BANCROFT

If one man can be singled out who contributed most to the establishment of the Naval Academy, that man is George Bancroft. He conciliated the older and younger elements of the Navy who could not agree as to whether midshipmen should be educated on shipboard or ashore and by June 6 had his plans so far advanced for a naval school that he felt ready to choose its site. To the Secretary of War on this day he wrote that a suitable place must be chosen with "the smallest expenditure of the public funds. From what I can learn of the position and accommodation of Fort Severn at Annapolis, I am inclined to think that that post would be a very suitable location." He then definitely asked Marcy for his co-operation in effecting a transfer of the post to the Navy. On the back of this brief letter is a still briefer endorsement in Marcy's hand: "I assent to the transfer 5 Aug. '45. W. L. Marcy." On June 13 Bancroft wrote to President Polk on the same subject. After outlining his proposal and the steps thus far taken he closed with: "I have the honor to solicit your authority for such transfer if the plan meets your approbation." Pasted on the back of the original of this letter of June 13 is an endorsement, apparently in Polk's handwriting. The endorsement is written on a small piece of yellow paper on which is printed in script: "The President of the United States." Polk's endorsement reads: "Secretary of the Navy. Proposing a transfer of Fort Severn from the Military to the Naval Service of the United States. No objection is perceived to the proposed transfer, the Secretary of War consenting thereto. June 16, 1845." By this very brief and simple exchange of correspondence the site was acquired for the greatest naval school on earth, and one will search in vain for any Act of Congress establishing the School. On August 15, 1845, the Adjutant General's Office in General Orders, No. 40, formally ordered Brevet Major J. L. Gardner, 4th Artillery, the Commanding Officer at Fort Severn, to transfer the fort to Commander Franklin Buchanan who had been designated by the Navy Department to take over the fort. But early in July, before Marcy had given his final consent, both he and Bancroft accompanied by Commodore Lewis Warrington visited Annapolis and accompanied by Major Gardner inspected the fort.

Bancroft now assembled a corps of instructors for his infant school. He chose Commander Franklin Buchanan, a stern disciplinarian and an educated and efficient officer, as the school's first Superintendent; to assist Buchanan, seven men were selected, three of whom, Lieut. James H. Ward, Professor William Chauvenet, and Professor Henry H. Lockwood, had made good records for themselves as instructors at the Philadelphia School. The others were Arsene N. Girault, instructor in French, Chaplain George Jones, instructor in English, Surgeon John A. Lockwood, instructor in Chemistry, and Passed Midshipman Samuel Marcy, assistant instructor in mathematics. Passed Midshipman Marcy, the son of the Secretary of War, was then ordered to proceed to West Point to inspect the system of training used at West Point and to make a full report on the Military Academy's curriculum. This report, signed by Marcy, and dated July 18, 1845, is now in the Museum of the Naval Academy.

The ceremonies by which the Naval School (it was not officially known as the U.S. Naval Academy until July 1, 1850) was formally opened were brief and simple. On Friday morning, October 10, 1845, at eleven o'clock the Superintendent assembled the officers, instructors, and midshipmen in one of the classrooms, read a letter from the Secretary of the Navy, and gave a brief address outlining the purpose for which the school was founded. Classes started at once. There were between fifty and sixty midshipmen in attendance. These students were formed into two classes: midshipmen who had never been to sea formed the junior class, or Youngsters; and midshipmen who had been to sea with but one year to go before taking their promotion examinations for Passed Midshipmen formed the senior class or Oldsters. The Youngsters were known officially as "Acting Midshipmen." To Cyrus H. Oakley, of New York, an acting midshipman, came the dubious honor of being the Naval Academy's first bilger who was "returned to his friends" on October 13. Mr. Oakley was but the first of a very long line of youths who sought a naval career and were thwarted in their desires by Academy officials who insisted on certain minimum standards of scholastic achievement.

In the Academy's early days smoking and card-playing were strictly taboo and no one thought it necessary to give these spirited youths a normal outlet for their exuberant spirits by providing athletic amusements. It was plainly up to the midshipmen to find such an outlet—to the detriment of the nerves of the Academic Board, the Superintendent, and the Commandant. They organized "supper clubs" which operated until all hours of the night. The nocturnal revels of the "Owls" and the "Crickets" stirred Annapolis to its very depths. They "frenched out" by scaling the walls, and rendezvousing at a popular saloon; the midshipmen inhabiting the "Abbey," a building close to the north wall, were, however, notably quiet and well-behaved. But one night the Officer of the Day entered the Abbey only to find it deserted. Its residents had found an intriguing tunnel under the wall in the basement and were using it to "french" out.

But they had some social diversions. In January, 1846, they held a naval ball in the Lyceum above the mess hall. They organized a theatrical company and in the spring of 1846 gave a play, "The Lady of Lyons" by Bulwer-Lytton. This play was given in a theater on Duke of Gloucester Street, shortly after purchased by the Presbyterian Church for their house of worship.

When the Civil War broke out, the Superintendent, Captain George S. Blake, with the approval of the Secretary of the Navy, removed the school to Newport, Rhode Island, where it remained during the four years of the war. The Navy Department rented a summer hotel known as the Atlantic House where the upper classes of midshipmen were quartered, the Plebes being housed on the *Constitution* anchored in the harbor of Newport. The Naval Academy grounds were taken over by the Army where a base hospital was established. This hospital took care of thousands of wounded troops returned from the battlefields of Virginia.

The outbreak of the Civil War 16 years after the official opening of the Naval School by Commander Buchanan found the Academy in a vastly improved situation. A four-year course was required of its students with practice cruises each summer. These students now came direct to the Academy from civil life and bore the cumbersome title of "Acting Midshipmen on probation at the Naval Academy." But the exigencies of war forced Congress to change this to "Midshipmen" in 1862. As "Acting Midshipmen" their status if captured in a practice ship by the Confederates was dubious. But the cartel or exchange value of a midshipman was definitely fixed, at that time, as equal to seven ordinary seamen or seven Army or Marine privates. By this same act of 1862 the grade of Passed Midshipman was abolished and the grade of Ensign substituted, a grade made equal to that of a Second Lieutenant in the Army or Marine Corps.

With the return of the Naval Academy from Newport on September 11, 1865, Vice Admiral David Dixon Porter, one of the outstanding Federal naval officers of the Civil War, took over as Superintendent. He modernized the curriculum, introduced new courses, brought in able young officers with war experience as instructors, cleaned up the grounds from the ravages made by the Army, constructed several new buildings, and introduced baseball, rowing, and other sports, affording the midshipmen the chance for athletic development that they long had needed. He so encouraged the Academy's social life that the newspaper wags of the period labeled the school "Porter's Dancing Academy."

Instead of being content with the simple graduation ceremonies of the past, he made the week of graduation a season of festivity with dances, parades, athletic events, and even introduced the competition for the company flag. Under his direction June Week became a week ever to be remembered in the life of the graduate, just as it is to this day. His force and energy gave new life to the school and most of his innovations are today standard procedure at the Academy.

For many years after the Civil War the Navy was moribund, the country not being interested in the Navy as a means of national defense in the piping times of peace. But under President Arthur the White Squadron was authorized and by the year 1898, when we went to war with Spain, we had a respectable naval force for that period. By June, 1897, 2,307 men had been graduated from the institution.

The short war with Spain had little effect on the Academy except that Admiral Cervera, the commander of the Spanish fleet destroyed at Santiago, with his officers were brought to the Academy as prisoners-of-war where they were quartered on what was then called Buchanan Row. They gave their parole not to leave the city but could go where they wished within the city's limits. They proved to be charming gentlemen and the city took great delight in feasting these most honorable foemen. After the conclusion of hostilities they left for their homes in Spain taking with them the good will of everyone.

During World War I the course was shortened to three years and the Naval Academy opened its doors to officers of the U.S. Naval Reserve who were given short courses in navigation, gunnery, seamanship, electrical and marine engineering, and Navy regulations and customs. During the course of the war the Academy supplied 2,569 Reserves for the naval service. In World War II the course was again shortened to three years and Reserve Midshipmen were again trained at the Academy. Since 1940, 4,138 regular midshipmen and 3,311 Reserve Midshipmen have been commissioned in the Navy and Marine Corps.

Over the years the midshipmen have developed a language of their own which would bewilder the chance visitor. His girl who comes to Annapolis for a Saturday night hop is his "drag," and if he is off with his girl for an afternoon's frolic he is "draggin'." Annapolis City is Crabtown and a girl who is a resident of the city is a "crab." A dignified member of the faculty possessed of a charming daughter who frequently entertained midshipmen friends was a guest at a midshipmen's banquet. He was startled to hear himself introduced in a most respectful manner by the toastmaster as "The Father of a well-known Annapolis crab." If a midshipman's name goes on the delinquency report for some midshipman sin, not necessarily connoting moral turpitude of any sort, he has been "fried" or "papped." If he should be so unfortunate as to go to sleep in the section room he "flaked out." The excellent food supplied him by the Commissary Department also comes in for strange appellations. Jello with whipped cream is "Shiverin' Liz in a snow storm," griddle cakes are "Collision mats," and stew, however good, is "slum" or "the mess cooks' holiday." If his passing mark is 2.5 or better, he is "sat," and if below he is "unsat." "Skinny" is the course given in Chemistry and Physics and the courses given by the dignified Department of English, History, and Government are affectionately and collectively known as "bull." Even the Superintendent is not let off. His title is shortened by his youthful midshipmen charges to "Supe," but obviously not in that gentleman's presence.

Fighting is forbidden but at times tempers flare and such rules are forgotten. It is also forbidden to prevaricate in the slightest degree. A midshipman with a black eye and a general dilapidated appearance sought the doctor in the Sick Bay. "What happened to you?" queried the genial doctor. "I might have run into a post," came the unexpected reply. "Come right in," said the man of medicine, "the post is here already." Talking in ranks is also forbidden. An officer queried a midshipman, "Did I just hear you talking in ranks?" "I sincerely hope not, sir." After a dubious recitation in Skinny a midshipman approached his instructor, "Do you think I deserved swabo for that recitation?" "No," his instructor replied, "but that is the lowest mark we give."

The officials of the Academy have often been criticized for not adding this or that new-fangled course to the curriculum. Sometimes men graduate from the Academy with no thought of making the Navy their career and resign at the first possible opportunity to take up civilian pursuits. A few of these men have complained that the Academy did not give them a "liberal" education. The answer to this criticism is simple and boiled down to its essence amounts to this:

The objective of Naval Academy education is twofold; first, to give a broad but functional basic and professional education on which the graduate may found his further study and training as a naval officer; second, to produce graduates capable of becoming efficient junior officers aboard ship in the shortest possible time.—(From the report of the Special Curriculum Committee appointed November, 1943, by the Superintendent, Rear Admiral John R. Beardall.)

If the complainant wanted an education in the classics or the fine arts he simply chose the wrong place.

But sometimes a bit of praise comes from a wholly unexpected source. The personnel manager of a large industrial concern in a near-by city had many requests for employment from Academy graduates who were forced to resign from the naval service because of impaired eyesight or some other physical defect. He had this to say of the product:

> There is one institution of higher learning in this country that has done more to solve this problem of personal development in its undergraduates than any I have encountered. Our proximity to Annapolis makes our office one of the first places to which prospective young naval graduates, who will not be commissioned because of failure to meet physical standards, turn when they learn that they will not be able to pursue their naval careers. I think I can say almost without exception, that these young men present a better front to the employer than the graduates of any other institution. They are poised, confident, assured, and courteous; they have that attitude of definite purpose which is a prized asset to a man in any walk of life.

Louis Bolander was Associate Librarian at the U.S. Naval Academy Library when he composed this article.

9 "Graduates of the U.S. Naval Academy"

Lieutenant William E. Wilson, USNR

U.S. Naval Institute *Proceedings*
(April 1946): 157–64

SINCE THE ESTABLISHMENT of the U.S. Naval Academy in 1845, the names of its graduates have become an integral part of the history of the United States. No school text in American history would be complete without inclusion of Admiral Dewey's victory at Manila, Admiral Sampson's achievement at Santiago, the exploits of "Fighting Bob" Evans, the explorations of Admiral Byrd, and the deeds of many others who have at one time or another worn the uniform of midshipmen at Annapolis. The magnificent achievements of such men are in no way disparaged or ignored here by the necessity of limiting a discussion of historic graduates of the Academy to those whose contributions to the service have been philosophical rather than dramatic, whose labors have made the traditions of education and training at Annapolis and in the fleet what they are today. Admirals Luce, Mahan, and Sims, whose names may not be so familiar to the general public as some others, personify in the minds of Navy men many of the standards that Annapolis now adheres to.

The Naval War College at Newport, Rhode Island, is in many ways a monument to the foresight and untiring determination of one of the Naval Academy's earliest graduates. Stephen Bleecker Luce was born in Albany, New York, in 1827, and at the age of fourteen, four years before the founding of the Academy, was appointed a midshipman in the fleet from New York. The *North Carolina*, the *Congress*, and the *Columbus* afforded him practical training for seven years before he was ordered to the Academy. He was graduated the next year with the rank of Passed Midshipman. During the early years of the Civil War, Luce was acting as head of the Academy's Department of Seamanship at Newport, where the institution was moved for safety in 1861; and it was during these years that he wrote his famous book *Seamanship*, for a long time the standard text on that subject. In 1865, however, Luce saw action in co-operating with General Sherman in the capture of Charleston. His next service at the Academy was as Commandant of Midshipmen under the lively and colorful regime of Admiral Porter. Luce finished his naval career in the rank of rear admiral, retiring in 1889.

Today at the Naval Academy, the building in which the Department of Seamanship and Navigation is housed bears the name of Rear Admiral Luce; but the memory of Luce is honored even more in the minds of Navy men for his great contribution to the education of officers. Luce, early in his career, realized that a naval officer's education should not stop on the day of his graduation from the Academy. At a time when the Navy was reduced and neglected, he constantly worked for the betterment of the service; and, convinced of the value of tactics and strategy, he put the ships he commanded through such rigorous and difficult maneuvers that officers under him frequently protested. Eventually his arguments for postgraduate study for officers broke down the indifference of seamen of the old school, and in 1884 an order was issued for the establishment of the Naval War College. Luce himself with the rank of commodore, was appointed first president of the college. There officers for sixty years have been receiving advanced instruction in history, international law, tactics, and strategy; and the college has become the model for similar institutions established in England, Germany, and Japan.

One of the lecturers on tactics and naval history whom Luce secured during his presidency of the Naval War College was Alfred Thayer Mahan.

Mahan, most widely famous of early graduates of the Naval Academy, was, paradoxically enough, born at West Point, the son of a professor of mathematics at the Military Academy. Before he entered the Naval Academy, he was a student for two years at Columbia University. At Annapolis, he made a brilliant record as a scholar, graduating second in the Class of 1859; but, because of his shy and studious nature and his rigid code of honor and correct manner, he was not very popular among his classmates. In the Civil War, he saw action at Port Royal and off Charleston. Thereafter, for twenty years, he led the life of any naval officer in peacetime, alternating between sea and shore duty and "drifting," as he himself wrote, "on the lines of simple respectability as aimlessly as anyone very well could."

It was Mahan's appointment as lecturer on tactics and naval history at the Naval War College and later his succession to the presidency of that institution that introduced him to the kind of work that was to make him internationally famous. In preparing for his lectures, Mahan laid the groundwork for his first great book, *The Influence of Sea Power upon History, 1660–1783,* which outlines the rise and fall of great maritime nations within the period and discusses the relationship of sea power to political history. This book and his later volume, *The Influence of Sea Power upon the French Revolution, 1793–1812,* which was published in 1892, were regarded first in Europe and later in the United States as the handbooks of colonial expansion. On a visit to England, Mahan was received by the Queen, and Kaiser Wilhelm II of Germany ordered his books placed on all German war vessels. President Theodore Roosevelt and Henry Cabot Lodge were strongly influenced by Mahan's doctrines, and in 1899 the Admiral was sent as a delegate to the first Hague Peace Conference, where he stood firmly opposed to international arbitration that might interfere with America's independence. He died in 1914 while preparing the material for a book on the relation of sea power to American expansion.

As Admirals Luce and Mahan labored for improvement in the education of naval officers, so Admiral William Sowden Sims brought about reforms in the training of men in the fleet. The headline in the *New York Times* of September 29, 1936, announcing Admiral Sims' death, describes him as the man who "taught the Navy how to shoot."

Sims was born in Ontario, Canada, in 1858, the son of American parents, and was graduated from the Naval Academy in 1880. His early years in the Navy, spent uneventfully aboard the *Philadelphia*, the *Charleston*, and the *Saratoga*, gave no hint of the tempestuous career that lay ahead of him, but in 1895 he began to send in reports from the China station criticizing the construction and the gunnery of American warships. "The Kentucky," he wrote bluntly at one time, "is not a battleship at all. She is the worst crime in naval construction ever perpetrated by the white race." For six years, Sims submitted adverse reports and they eventually piled up to the grand total of 11,000 pages; at the end of that time, in November, 1901, he wrote directly to President Roosevelt, apologizing for going over the heads of his superiors, but pointing out that he was calling the chief executive's attention to his unheeded reports in the interest of the U.S. Navy. The result was a tempest in the White House and the Navy Department. "Give Sims entire charge of target practice for eighteen months," President Roosevelt is reported to have ordered. "Do exactly as he says. If he does not accomplish something in that time, cut off his head and try somebody else." That Sims lived to command American naval operations in European waters during World War I is sufficient proof that, under President Roosevelt's order, he "accomplished" something.

Admiral Sims' contribution to the philosophy of the Navy was that of a relentless and courageous critic, rather than a formulator of large policies. He criticized and reformed American naval construction and gunnery; he spoke out bluntly about American foreign policy; he attacked the system of training at Annapolis and the system of promotion in the Navy itself. He was often at outs with his colleagues. But he was respected by all who knew him, and on the day of his death, fourteen years after his retirement, some of the men whom he excoriated most severely joined in his praises.

The list of famous men in the uniform of the United States Navy has grown to enormous proportions since Pearl Harbor. The names of Halsey, Spruance, Hewitt, Kirk, Ingersoll, Turner, Mitscher, and many others are familiar to every school boy in America. Full justice to the graduates of the Naval Academy who have brought glory to their country and their alma mater in the present conflict would require volumes, for such an account should not be limited only to men of admiral's rank but should include many on whose ensign's commissions the ink is hardly dry. To economize in space, this account must be limited to the three contemporary naval officers who have achieved the distinction of becoming five-star admirals; but it should be understood that a tribute to them is an implied tribute to the many thousands of others of all ranks who have fought and are still fighting in World War II, for, without their courage and loyalty, the distinguished labors of Admirals Leahy, King, and Nimitz alone would be of no avail.

Admiral Ernest Joseph King, Commander in Chief of the United States Fleet and Chief of Naval Operations, learned to fly at the age of forty-nine; and it is that spirit of modernity and aggressiveness which has raised him to the most powerful position ever held by an officer in the United States Navy. Admiral King was born in Ohio in 1878 and was graduated fourth in scholastic standing in the Naval Academy class of 1901. During World War I, he was assistant chief of staff to the Commander in Chief of the Atlantic Fleet, and at the close of the war he superintended the reopening of the Postgraduate School at Annapolis. In 1933, President Roosevelt, discovering that no admiral in the Navy knew how to fly, took Captain King from his billet as skipper of the *Lexington* and made him chief of the Bureau of Aeronautics. In 1938, he became vice admiral in command of the Aircraft Battle Force. Two years later, he was made an admiral and given command of the Atlantic Fleet, and in 1941 he assumed his post as commander in chief.

The tradition of the U.S. Navy is and always has been that a naval officer should be well versed in all departments of his duties and capable of undertaking any assignment given to him ashore and afloat. In an age of specialization, it has become more and more difficult to uphold this tradition; yet Admiral King, a submariner, a flyer, and a commander of surface ships, has proved, in his own person, that nothing is impossible. He has been, therefore, in large part, responsible for the teamwork and the modern aggressive spirit of the U.S. Navy in its time of severest trial. Always a stern disciplinarian, he has imbued his service with the same spirit that he himself exhibits.

Since 1942, Admiral William Daniel Leahy has occupied the position of Chief of Staff to the Commander in Chief of the Army and Navy of the United States, the first man in history to hold such a position. Born in Iowa in 1875, Admiral Leahy was graduated from the Naval Academy in 1897. He undertook his first service during the Philippine Insurrection in the Spanish-American War. He was chief of staff of the Nicaragua occupation in 1912 and of the Haitian campaign in 1916 and attained the rank of captain during World War I. With the rank of rear admiral, he headed the Bureau of Ordnance and the Bureau of Navigation and was Chief of Naval Operations upon his retirement in 1939. In that year, he was appointed governor of Puerto Rico and was later made ambassador to France before being called back to active duty in his present position.

A student, a quiet, reflective man, Admiral Leahy has distinguished himself as a man who is always prepared for his next assignment. Those who work with him always remark upon his studiousness, his intense concentration upon the job in hand during working hours and upon the job just ahead during his leisure time.

The third of our five-star admirals held during the war the title of Commander in Chief of the U.S. Pacific Fleet. He is Chester William Nimitz, born in Texas in 1885 and a graduate of the Naval Academy in the Class of 1905. A few years thereafter, he was given command of a submarine and eventually became commander of the Atlantic Submarine Flotilla. In submarines during World War I and frequently since that time, his career was chiefly one of commands afloat until, on December 17, 1941, he undertook the highly important job of directing the naval war in the Pacific. A man unselfishly devoted at all times to his duty and in love with his profession, Admiral Nimitz is noted throughout the fleet for the personal loyalty that he inspires in the men who work under him. A natural leader, an intuitive judge of men, he exemplifies the U.S. naval officer at his best.

The Naval Academy is thought of only as an institution designed for the training of officers in the U.S. Navy, and that, of course is its sole purpose. Yet men who have been retired from the Navy or who have resigned in peaceful times when there was but a limited opportunity for officers to advance have proved that the basic training at the Academy is a sound preparation for success in other activities than those of the Navy. Many civilians have reflected credit on their alma mater in Annapolis.

Graduates of the Naval Academy who resign from the Navy to become educators usually turn to the sciences because of the nature of their training at Annapolis. Robert Lee Flowers, of the Class of 1891, although he became a professor of mathematics at Duke University after resigning his commission, is an exception to the rule. Since 1941, he has been president of Duke and his additional offices as president of the South Atlantic Publishing Company, director of the Durham and South-ern Railway Company, and trustee of Greensboro College testify to the breadth of his interests.

Professor William Frederick Durand, who served in the Engineering Corps of the Navy for seven years after his graduation from the Academy in 1880, is another alumnus who, though his principal interest has been mechanical engineering, has participated in a wide variety of intellectual and social activities. For four years professor of mechanical engineering at the Agricultural and Mechanical College of Michigan, for thirteen years professor of marine engineering at Cornell University, and for twenty years professor of mechanical engineering at Leland Stanford, Jr., Uni-versity, he is now a professor emeritus of the last institution he served. Professor Durand's horizon, however, has not been limited to the class-room. To list only a few of his broader activities, he has been scientific attaché at the American Embassy in Paris, a member of the Interallied Committee on Inventions, a member of the advisory board of engineers of the Boulder Dam Project, and a member of the American Academy of Sciences, and has won many medals for research and experiment.

The Naval Academy has produced three successive presidents of Worcester Polytechnic Institute. Ira N. Hollis, who was graduated in 1878 and resigned in 1893, served an apprenticeship for that office for ten years in the chair of engineering at Harvard University. In 1913 he became the president of Worcester and held that office for twelve years. He was succeeded by another Academy man, Ralph Earle. Earle, of the Class of 1896, who held the rank of rear admiral upon his retirement, experienced thirty years of active and productive service in the Navy before he became a professional educator. He saw action in the Spanish-American War and World War I, but his great claim to fame in the Navy is that as wartime head of the Bureau of Ordnance he put through the mine field across the North Sea in World War I and he promoted plans for depth charges later developed to such effectiveness in the present war. Successor to Admiral Earle and present incumbent at Worcester is Admiral Wat Tyler Cluverius, who also was graduated from the Academy in 1896. Admiral Cluverius served actively and in many capacities in the Navy for forty-three years before retiring.

It is not surprising that graduates of the Academy who resign to become journalists and writers should devote their literary talents to naval affairs. Hanson W. Baldwin, whose columns and articles in newspapers and magazines have guided the thinking of many readers in World War II, graduated in 1924 and served for three years aboard battleships and a destroyer before resigning to become police reporter for the *Baltimore Sun*. Since 1942, the year in which he was awarded a Pulitzer Prize, he has been military editor of the *New York Times*. Herbert Paul Schubert, journalist and lecturer, author of *Sea Power in Conflict*, is another Academy man who has become an authority on naval affairs. He was graduated in 1919 and retired in 1924. The Literary Guild selection of *On the Bottom* in 1929 brought fame as a writer to Edward

Ellsberg, who was graduated first in the Class of 1914 at the Academy and served for twelve years before resigning. He is now on active duty in the Naval Reserve as a captain. Others of his books that have reached a large public are *Hell on Ice* and *Captain Paul*. No list of Naval Academy authors would be complete without the name of Winston Churchill, who was graduated in 1894 and resigned the same year. The famous author of *Richard Carvel, The Crisis*, and *The Inside of the Cup* sold his first short story to Century two years after graduation, and his list of publications is now of very impressive proportions.

Although politics is a subject that plays a very small role in the life of a midshipman and a naval officer, the Naval Academy has produced its share of men who have succeeded in political life. At least two cabinet members, three senators, two ambassadors, and a representative in Congress are notable among them. John Wingate Weeks, of the Class of 1881, once a member of Hornblower and Weeks in Boston, and later a representative and then a senator, served as Secretary of War in the cabinets of Presidents Harding and Coolidge. Curtis Dwight Wilbur, Class of 1888, whose midshipman record in the hop, skip, and jump incidentally still stands, studied law after resigning from the Navy and eventually became Chief Justice of the Supreme Court of California, from which seat he resigned to become President Coolidge's Secretary of the Navy. The Academy's two senators, besides Weeks, are R. Beecher Howell of the Class of 1885, who served two terms from Nebraska, and Admiral Thomas Charles Hart, of the Class of 1897, who was recently appointed senator from Connecticut. Admiral Leahy's services as ambassador to France have already been mentioned. Admiral William Harrison Standley, who graduated in 1895, was appointed ambassador to the U.S.S.R. shortly after his retirement from the Navy and served in that capacity during the crucial period 1942–43. A member of the House of Representatives since 1937, Edouard Victor Michel Izac is a graduate of the Class of 1915. He was on active duty in the Navy for twenty-one years before entering Congress, and made a daring escape from a German prison camp in World War I.

In the 1920s when, because of the reduction in the size of the Navy, officers were encouraged to resign, representatives of large corporations visited Annapolis to interview members of the graduating classes. They had found and they were frequently quoted as saying that graduates of the Naval Academy were valuable assets in any business firm because Navy men were trained in loyalty and co-operation and their discipline stood them in good stead in business. To list all the graduates of the Academy who have succeeded in business would be an endless undertaking. Four men, therefore, may be taken as representative.

Joseph Wright Powell was graduated in the Class of 1897. He served in the Spanish-American War, was later sent to study at the University of Glasgow, and finally resigned his commission in 1906. In 1914, he became president of the Fore River Shipbuilding Corporation. Utilizing his experience and prestige in this business when we entered World War I, he organized the five shipyards of the Bethlehem Steel Corporation, which in 1917 had undertaken the greater part of the Navy's destroyer program. He was for a time thereafter president of the United States Shipbuilding Emergency Fleet Corporation. During the present conflict, he has been special assistant to the Secretary of Navy and deputy chief of the office of Procurement and Material.

Homer Lenoir Ferguson's career as a shipbuilder has closely paralleled Mr. Powell's. Graduated from the Academy in 1892, he too studied at the University of Glasgow. He holds several honorary degrees from such institutions as the University of Richmond, Duke University, and Worcester Polytechnic Institute. Since 1905, he has been with the Newport News Shipbuilding and Drydock Company, as president and general manager from 1915 to 1937, and as chairman of the board and president since 1938. His services in the last two wars have contributed greatly to the speed and magnitude that have characterized our shipbuilding programs.

The name of Deering is familiar to anyone who has spent any of his life on a farm during the past fifty years. Charles Deering, of the Class of 1873, resigned in 1881 to become secretary of the Deering Harvester Company, and he served for many years as chairman of the board of the International Harvester Company when it was merged with the Deering firm.

Sidney Zollicoffer Mitchell, one of the originators of the modern holding company, is a name familiar to all who have followed the activities of big business during the past half century. He was graduated from the Academy in 1883 and resigned from the service after two years. Once chairman of the board of Electric Bond and Share, Mr. Mitchell was for many years associated with public utilities.

Above all else, the Naval Academy is famous for the scientists and engineers it has produced; and, although many of the men already mentioned are or have been scientists in their own right, it might be well to round out the list with three famous names—McFarland, Sprague, and Michelson.

Walter Martin McFarland, Class of 1879, resigned in 1899 and became vice-president of the Westinghouse Electric Company. Later he was manager of the marine department of the Babcock and Wilcox Company. His great distinction in the history of the Navy is that in 1890 he was the first to propose that the speed of ships on contract trials might be determined by the curve of speed and engine revolutions obtained on progressive trials on a measured mile.

Frank J. Sprague, who resigned five years after his graduation in 1878, founded the Sprague Electric Railway and Motor Company, famous for many "firsts" in transportation and electrical science, among them the first modern trolley railway in the United States at Richmond, Virginia. Sprague himself invented the multiple unit system train control and engaged for years in promoting underground rapid transit.

Albert Abraham Michelson, the famous physicist, 1852–1931, was born in Germany. His parents brought him to this country when he was two years old and eventually were attracted by the gold rush to California and later to Nevada. Michelson, by great tenacity of purpose, obtained an appointment to the Naval Academy through the influence of the Commandant of Midshipmen after failing in interviews with his Congressman and President Grant. Graduating from the Academy in 1873, he later served for four years as an instructor in physics and chemistry. After further study in Berlin, Heidelberg, and Paris, he was a professor for many years at the Case School of Applied Science and Clark University and ultimately head of the Department of Physics in the University of Chicago. Professor Michelson's fame, however, is not dependent upon his career as an educator but upon his scientific career, begun while he was still a midshipman. That career is associated with the word "light." His experiments with light fall into two departments: the determination of the velocity of light and the study of optical interference. With apparatus of his own design and construction at a cost of less than ten dollars, he first measured the speed of light while at Annapolis. He continued to refine and perfect this original experiment throughout the remainder of his life and for this one achievement more than any other his name is of classic importance in the history of science.

10 "Naval Academy Memories"

*Jeremiah Denton, James L. Holloway III,
Charles R. Larson, James A. Lovell,
John J. McMullen, Thomas H. Moorer,
Oliver L. North, John M. Poindexter, David Poyer,
Alan B. Shepard Jr., Roy C. Smith, Roger Staubach,
Stansfield Turner, and James H. Webb Jr.*

Naval History (October 1995): 8–16

NAVAL HISTORY salutes the 150th anniversary of the U.S. Naval Academy with these remembrances from 14 distinguished alumni, all having made notable contributions in military and government service, business, sports, or literature. Each of our correspondents answered the following question: "What was your most memorable experience at the U.S. Naval Academy?"

Jeremiah Denton, Class of 1947

My most memorable experiences at the Naval Academy were enhanced by the benefit of my association with my brilliant roommate, Donald B. Wenger, who later was nosed out by classmate Pat March as head of the Naval Security Group. Don has been an inspiration to me all my life.

Misery loves company, and my very rugged plebe year was made easier by two classmates, Bob Gatewood and Skip Steloff, sharing in my enslavement to a particular first-classman who decided that the three of us really needed shaping up. Of course, he was dead right and made a career of it all year.

My greatest triumphs were being the first plebe to climb the Herndon Monument, signaling the end of plebedom for the Class of 1947, and passing the final examination in Navigation with a 3.98 under the pressure of my future wife, family, and friends in Annapolis for our wedding, which would not have happened if my exam had been as bad as my daily grade.

My greatest satisfaction is the endurance of intense relationships with classmates like Wenger, Gatewood, Swoose Snead, Jim Stockdale, and Jim Wilson (my last boss in the Navy in 1977, my company commander at the Academy, and my administrative assistant in the Senate).

Retired Rear Admiral Denton is active in the National Forum Foundation, which he founded in 1983. As a U.S. Senator from Alabama, he chaired the Subcommittee on Security and Terrorism and the Subcommittee on Aging, Family, and Human Services and served on the Senate Armed Services and Veterans Affairs committees. During the Vietnam War, he spent seven years and seven months—four in solitary confinement—as a prisoner of war. He is perhaps best remembered for his televised interview from Hanoi in 1966, when he spelled out "torture" in Morse code by blinking his eyes.

James L. Holloway III, Class of 1943

The time was a pleasant Sunday morning in May 1942. In the Pacific, Corregidor had just fallen to the Japanese, and gas rationing had been instituted in the United States the week before. The place was Leutze Park in the yard of the Naval Academy. It was a bittersweet moment. I was sitting on a bench on Youngster Cut-off, across from the chapel with my drag, Dabney Rawlings (today my wife of 53 years), saying goodbye. In a few minutes I would head for noon formation at Bancroft Hall and Dabney for the bus depot to take the Greyhound back to college in Philadelphia.

It had been a wonderful weekend. Dabney had come down for the hop on Saturday night—long formals for the girls and full dress for the mids. There was no drinking, no riding in cars—both proscribed with the threat of expulsion—and even the first classmen like myself had to be checked back into our bunks in Bancroft one hour after the hop ended at 2330. Sunday morning we had attended chapel—compulsory—and then walked in the yard, because liberty outside the gates did not start, even for first-classmen, until after noon formation.

The time together meant a lot to us. In less than a month, I would be an ensign on my way to the war on board a destroyer in the Pacific. As we got up to go our respective ways, Dabney to her bus and me to muster my platoon, I reached over to clasp one of her hands in both of mine as I told her how much I looked forward to seeing her June Week.

Suddenly, at this moment, out of the bushes behind us rushed a Jimmy Legs—a civilian campus cop—with his pad and paper ready. "Mister, what is your name? You are on the report for P.D.A. (public display of affection)." That single indiscretion caused me to be confined to my room for the next weekend. As my Company Commander said, "As a first classman, soon to be an officer, you should set a better example." Whew!

Retired Admiral Holloway is President of the Naval Historical Foundation. He was the 20th Chief of Naval Operations immediately before retiring in 1978. He served in three wars, beginning with World War II, and received three Navy Distinguished Service Medals and two Defense Distinguished Service Medals. A naval aviator, he was captain of the first nuclear-powered aircraft carrier, the USS Enterprise (CVAN-65).

Charles R. Larson, Class of 1958

One of my most memorable experiences at the Naval Academy as a midshipman happened in the fall of 1957. Navy played Army in the first-ever

meeting of our two 150-pound football teams. We played in the old
Thompson Stadium, and the First Regiment conducted a march-on. The
proceeds from the game went to a fund for our new Navy-Marine Corps
Memorial Stadium.

What made the game memorable was the presence of our Commander-
in-Chief, President Dwight D. Eisenhower, a West Point alumnus. As
Brigade Commander, I greeted him on behalf of the Brigade, and he presented me with a historic Viking sword, which I accepted on behalf of
the Naval Academy. This was the first time I had ever met a President.
Little did I dream that by the 150th anniversary of the Naval Academy,
I would have met and had significant conversations with every President
from Truman to Clinton, except John F. Kennedy. Also, as Naval Aide
to President Nixon, I was with Mrs. Mamie Eisenhower at Walter Reed
Hospital the night that General Eisenhower died.

> **Admiral Larson** is in his second tour as Superintendent of the U.S.
> Naval Academy. Both a naval aviator and a nuclear submariner, he
> was the 15th U.S. naval officer to hold the position of Commander-
> in-Chief, U.S. Pacific Command, before his return to the helm at
> Annapolis. Admiral Larson's decorations include six Distinguished
> Service Medals, three Legions of Merit, a Bronze Star, the Navy
> Commendation Medal and the Navy Achievement Medal.

James A. Lovell Jr., Class of 1952

My most memorable event at the Naval Academy happened during my
first-class year—but it was not memorable at the time.

Rockets and space travel fascinated me as a boy. I devoured all the
information on rocket technology, including the works of Robert God-
dard and Wernher von Braun. I wanted to pursue a career in rocket engineering when I graduated high school, but I could not afford the colleges.
I was fortunate to be appointed to the Naval Academy, and that secured
my education. But I still had a love for rockets.

One of the requirements first-class year was to research and write a term paper on a military subject—usually some aspect of military history. I chose to write on the development of the liquid-fueled rocket engine. My girlfriend (now my wife) typed the paper but warned me that a non-military subject might adversely affect my grade.

I still remember the last paragraph: "The big day for rockets is still coming, the day when science will have advanced to the stage when flight into space is a reality and not a dream."

Ten years later, I was preparing for my first space mission.

Retired Captain Lovell was commander of the ill-fated Apollo 13 mission, which is depicted in the highly popular summer 1995 film by the same name. Actor Tom Hanks plays the quick-witted Lovell, who recently received the Congressional Space Medal of Honor— for heroism in bringing the severely damaged spacecraft safely back to earth—from President Bill Clinton.

John J. McMullen, Class of 1940

As a young man more than 65 years ago, I met Royce Flippin from the Class of 1926. From that point, all through my high school career, I dreamed of the Academy and did not even take the time to look at any other single institution of higher education.

Entering the Academy on 9 July 1936 began a series of experiences that remain in my memory. While these experiences were not always pleasant (walking off demerits, push-ups, grilling in the Mess Hall, trembling before commissioned officers), the Academy prepared me academically, militarily, and athletically, forming my character and personality for the rest of my life.

During the last four years of the 1930s, being at the Naval Academy was a dream. Midshipmen cruises in the summer, competitive sports, and forming life-long friendships and fellowships were some of my best memories. I cannot imagine having been educated at any other college in the United States. The years were filled completely with activity. The competition in each and every one of those activities formed the basis for determination, leadership, and achievement.

At this stage, I regret that I can never repeat those four years. I have been fortunate in being able to continue a modest association with many of the Superintendents and the Academy in general. My decision back in the '30s was no doubt correct, because after exposure to many other institutions of higher learning, I truly believe the U.S. Naval Academy is still the finest college in the country. Nowhere else can a young man or woman experience education plus leadership and practical experience.

> **Mr. McMullen** is Majority Owner and Chairman of the 1995 National Hockey League Stanley Cup Champion New Jersey Devils and Owner and Director of Norton Lilly International, Inc., general international shipping agents for more than 150 years. He is also Chairman of John J. McMullen Associates, Inc., a division of Talley Industries, Inc., and former Majority Owner and Chairman of Major League Baseball's Houston Astros.

Thomas H. Moorer, Class of 1933

As I look back over 62 years, during which I fought in three wars and also participated in several lesser conflicts, my most memorable experience at the Naval Academy was not a single event but a continuous series of events that clearly indicated my primary interest, naval aviation, was receiving progressive attention. For the first time, during my second-class summer, Douglas Flying Boats were flown from the fleet units for flight operations in the Severn River. All members of our class were given indoctrination flights as well as lectures on fleet employment of aircraft of all types including from our three carriers.

An extremely interesting and thought-provoking time was enjoyed by my math class; thanks to a very imaginative professor, Dr. William

Conrad. On occasion, he would simply ignore the lesson of the day and instruct the class in the mathematics involved in flying to the moon. Dr. Conrad certainly stimulated my imagination. He said all we needed was a big rocket. About 30 years later, it happened, and large numbers of the astronauts were naval aviators.

The Class of 1933 used naval aviation as the theme of the 1933 *Lucky Bag* yearbook, and the class ring I have worn for more than 60 years has above the Academy seal an aircraft radial engine, complete with propeller. Naval aviation was on the way, and at the Battle Midway in June 1942 it reversed the course of the War in the Pacific. Today, when faced with a military crisis overseas, the first question still asked by the National Security Council is: "Where are the carriers?"

> **Retired Admiral Moorer** served as the 18th Chief of Naval Operations under President Lyndon B. Johnson and was reappointed by President Richard M. Nixon, under whom he later served two consecutive terms as Chairman of the Joint Chiefs of Staff. His distinguished and lengthy career as a naval aviator and leader included the distinction of being the only naval officer ever to have commanded both the Pacific and Atlantic Fleets.

Oliver L. North, Class of 1968

Memories from "the Academy" after more than two-and-one-half decades are highly subjective. My most vivid recollections are not so much of events, but of people—classmates who shared the ordeal, professors, instructors and officers who tried to teach us, and of course, the upperclass who harassed us. But no one stands out so much in my recall as Emerson Smith, the legendary boxing coach.

I especially liked boxing because whether you won or lost, there was no one else to blame. For those of us with no natural ability as pugilists, Coach Smith reduced boxing to a few basic rules. To this day, I can hear his voice booming above the staccato slap of the speed bags and the heavier thud of fists pounding the heavy bags in the sweaty basement of Macdonough Hall: "Keep your hands up, your feet moving, and your ass off the deck! If you get knocked down, get back up, dust yourself off, and get back in the fight! Go get 'em! Don't give up! The fight's not over 'till the final bell!"

Coach Smith was, of course, right. Interestingly enough, his advice works as well in life as it did in the boxing ring.

> **Retired Marine Lieutenant Colonel North** is currently host of his own syndicated radio talk program, "The Oliver North Show." In 1994, he ran unsuccessfully in Virginia against Charles Robb (D-VA) for the U.S. Senate. Colonel North served on the National Security Council under President Ronald Reagan.

John M. Poindexter, Class of 1958

The 4th of June 1958 dawned bright and clear, and the Class of '58 was ending the first phase of their careers and getting ready to start the second. The graduation ceremonies were to be held in the new Field House, and President Dwight D. Eisenhower was to deliver the graduation address. My class had marched in President Eisenhower's second inaugural parade on a bitter cold day in January 1957 after his landslide victory. I cannot remember what he said in his graduation address, but I am certain he intended it to be inspirational. For me it was inspirational just to have a remote association with this great military leader of World War II and the leader of the Free World. After the address, the President presented the diplomas. As I led the class to the stage steps, my knees were shaking. As the President handed me my diploma and grasped my hand in a firm grip, he said, "Congratulations, Mr. Poindexter. I hope it won't be too much of a burden for you."

Years later, when I was serving President Ronald Reagan in the White House, I often reflected on the prophetic nature of his comment.

Retired Rear Admiral Poindexter is Senior Scientist for Presearch, Inc., and cofounder of TP Systems, Inc., a computer software developer. After a distinguished career in the U.S. Navy, he served as Deputy National Security Advisor and National Security Advisor to President Ronald Reagan.

David Poyer, Class of 1971

I reached the Academy from a childhood passed on welfare. As Randall Jarrell has it, "From my mother's sleep I fell into the State." My most enduring memory is of a Hundredth Night buildup so intense I went into temporary amnesia during a come-around. Plebe Year remains seared not only on my memory, but on my personality. Since I appeared devoid of command presence and leadership ability, my upperclassmen went all out to relieve the Navy of me. Nine months of physical and psychological stress at the age of 17 had lasting results. I had to write a novel to externalize and escape some of them. Some are positive: self-confidence and self-control, a coolness that emerges when things are going to hell all around. Others are less admirable: a tendency to focus on the goal rather than the people involved; a certain ruthlessness; a loyalty to the group that I persist in past the point of sense. A quarter-century later I still puzzle over this equivocal legacy. Without it I would be a different person. But who? Less effective? Kinder? Less inclined to arrogance? Perhaps there is no final answer. Only the one in the mirror, every day.

Mr. Poyer is a novelist living on Virginia's Eastern Shore. He has written some 16 books, including *The Return of Philo T. McGiffin*, a novel of Annapolis; *The Med*, *The Gulf*, and *The Circle*, bestselling Navy novels; and *Hatteras Blue*, *Bahamas Blue*, and *Louisiana Blue*, all underwater adventures.

Alan B. Shepard Jr., Class of 1945

A couple of things come to mind in answer to this question. The first memorable experience was plebe year and the fact that I was able to make it through at all. I say this very seriously, because I was relatively young when I came to the Academy. I had gone through a rural school system (East Derry, New Hampshire), where I had been a big fish in a small pond. I had done very well in school—even skipped a couple of grades. Of course, I was delighted when I received the appointment. But life had been too easy for me before I came to the Academy. I had not had to work very hard in school, and all of a sudden, boom—I was competing with some of the nation's best. Plebe year—which included hazing in those days—was just overwhelming, and it took me the better part of that year to get organized and cranked around. I was so glad when it was over. Then things improved, obviously.

The other thing I remember most vividly is that I was a pretty scrawny guy. I tried football, but I was just too small. Then I got involved in crew and was able to be on the varsity crew in 1944. We had a good season, and I earned my "N."

I also must mention how pleasing it is to me—and it should be to everybody in the Navy—that, in the astronaut business, the performance of naval officers has been remarkably above and beyond contributions from any other source. Five out of the six commanders who landed on the moon were Navy pilots. The two guys who flew the first shuttle were Navy pilots. The first guy in space was a Navy pilot. The first to orbit the earth was a Marine, Navy-trained. The first guy to land and walk on the moon was a Navy pilot. It's an incredible accomplishment, and we ought to be proud of it.

Retired Rear Admiral Shepard is president of the Houston-based Seven Fourteen Enterprises, Inc., and the Mercury Seven Foundation. He became the first American to fly in space on 5 May 1961 and was commander of the Apollo 14 mission to the moon nearly ten years later. He is the coauthor of *Moon Shot: The Inside Story of America's Race to the Moon* (Atlanta: Turner Publishing, Inc., 1994).

Roy C. Smith III, Class of 1934

Sixty-odd years ago, candidates entered the Academy daily in small groups of 20 or so rather than by today's all-in-one I-Day. In late June of 1930 I took the oath of office as a midshipman along with about two dozen others in Memorial Hall under Commodore Oliver Hazard Perry's Lake Erie flag. Considering that I thus became the sixth generation of Navy in the family, that was a very memorable event in itself. An older gentleman stood erect nearby, white-headed but with a twinkle in his eye. He looked familiar, I thought. When the oath-taking ceremony was finished, the Commandant introduced the old-timer as Admiral William S. Sims, Commander Naval Forces Europe in the World War, and asked him to give us a few words of wisdom. He would be delighted. He spoke briefly and concisely, but now I remember only his closing remark. The Admiral said that the most important thing he had learned in his long career was patience, a virtue much to be desired. I wondered how the Navy had taught patience. He paused, looked us over, and said, "I spent 40 years in the Navy, 30 of them waiting for boats."

> **Retired Captain Smith** writes frequently for U.S. Naval Institute publications. The former editor of *Shipmate* and Director of Publications for the U.S. Naval Academy Alumni Association, he saw extensive Navy service in five ships. Captain Smith also served for four years as Director of the U.S. Navy Museum in Washington, D.C.

Roger Staubach, Class of 1965

My experience at the Naval Academy influenced my life in so many ways, but Rear Admiral Charles Kirkpatrick made a major impression on me. He was a charismatic leader, and the example I would like to relate was connected to varsity football.

At each pep rally, the Admiral would speak and he would end it with, "You can do anything you want to do if you make up your mind to do it!" During my junior year at Annapolis, we had a successful season winning football games, and there was a lot of excitement at the rallies. The Brigade would chant, "We want Uncle Charlie, we want Uncle Charlie," at which time he would rise to the occasion with "You can do anything. . . ." and the whole Brigade would mouth it ahead of him or along with him.

Admiral Kirkpatrick's message embodied more than the enthusiasm of the moment. It characterized the value of teamwork for a football player, a naval officer, a businessman. What an important message to communicate to the troops—respect others, give your best effort to the task at hand, and you have the winning formula.

As I moved from the Navy to professional football to the business world, "You can do anything you want to do if you make up your mind to do it!" has been my mantra.

> **Mr. Staubach** is Chairman of the Board and Chief Executive Officer of The Staubach Company of Dallas, Texas, specializing in corporate and professional real estate. Inducted into the Pro Football Hall of Fame in 1985, he led the Dallas Cowboys to four Super Bowls and two Super Bowl victories. In his second-class year at the Naval Academy, he received the Heisman Trophy, and he is the only midshipman ever to win the Thompson Trophy Cup for best all-around athlete, three years in a row.

Stansfield Turner, Class of 1947

"Midshipman First Class Turner, Mr. Secretary. Welcome to the Naval Academy." It was May 1946 on Worden Field. Secretary of the Navy James V. Forrestal had just reviewed our weekly Wednesday afternoon parade. From under his broad-brimmed fedora, Forrestal barked to me, "Turner, I understand you want to be a Rhodes Scholar." Taken aback, I stumbled out with, "Yes, sir, but the Navy has a regulation against officers competing for Rhodes Scholarships." The course of my life was about to change.

This had all started a few weeks before, when I had arranged an appointment with the Commandant of Midshipman to ask whether he thought the regulation in question could be changed. About an hour later he called me back to his office, where he introduced me to Mr. Ferdinand Eberstadt, Chairman of the Secretary of the Navy's Board of Visitors to the Naval Academy that year. James Collier, a classmate, came in on my heels. The Commandant then left, saying Mr. Eberstadt wanted to chat privately with a couple of midshipmen.

It was an uneventful discussion until Mr. Eberstadt said, "Turner, the Commandant tells me you want to be a Rhodes Scholar." "Yes, sir," I replied, "but the Navy has a regulation against it." He assured me he would talk to the "Secretary" about it. I immediately thought he meant the Secretary of the Board of Visitors. But I soon learned that Eberstadt was a long-time confidant of James Forrestal.

Out on the parade field, the Secretary turned to the Vice Admiral on his left, Louis E. Denfeld, the Chief of Naval Personnel. "Louis, I think we ought to change that regulation." The regulation was changed. I competed, won, and went on to Oxford. And the Navy has had 25 Rhodes Scholars in the years since—thanks to James V. Forrestal.

Retired Admiral Turner was Director of the Central Intelligence Agency in the Carter administration. He also served as President of the Naval War College and as Commander-in-Chief, Allied Forces Southern Europe.

James H. Webb Jr., Class of 1968

The Vietnam War began in earnest for the United States during the Class of 1968's plebe summer, and international conflict consumed our midshipman experience, both at the Academy and during our cruises. We spent our youngster cruise ferrying troops, ammunition, and supplies between California and Hawaii, on their way to Vietnam. My first-class cruise in the Mediterranean began one day after the 1967 Arab-Israeli

War, when the *Saratoga* (CVA-60) medevaced casualties from the USS *Liberty* (AGTR-5) and saw the Soviet fleet move full-time into the Med. The North Koreans captured the USS *Pueblo* (AGER-2) during our first-class year. We held service-selection as the Tet Offensive raged. Television coverage of the Marine Corps—which ended up taking more casualties in Vietnam than even in World War II—was prominent and bloody. As a result, ours was the first class in memory not to fill its Marine Corps quota. In my battalion alone, 11 of the 22 "confirmed" future Marines opted for other billets.

But as one might expect, a strong percentage of those who chose the Corps were unusually dedicated and prepared for what was expected of them. The five ground officers among the six battalion "coordinators" accounted for nine Purple Hearts, including one killed in action. And of the 81 midshipmen who stepped forward on that bleak night, six already have become general officers.

Mr. Webb is a producer and screenwriter and president of his own production company. A highly decorated Marine Corps veteran of the Vietnam War, he has written four novels, won an Emmy Award for his coverage of U.S. Marines in Beirut in 1983, and served as Secretary of the Navy in the Reagan administration from 1987 to 1988.

11 "Naval Academy Memories"

Edward L. Beach, Jimmy Carter,
John H. Dalton, John S. McCain III,
Robert C. McFarlane, Walter M. Schirra

U.S. Naval Institute *Proceedings*
(October 1995): 38–41

IN HONOR OF the 150th anniversary of the U.S. Naval Academy, *Proceedings* presents six of the venerable institution's distinguished alumni and their answers to the question: "What was your most memorable experience at the U.S. Naval Academy?"

Edward L. Beach, Class of 1939

Study hours had just begun on Halloween night of 1938, and I held the august title of Regimental Commander. Although first classmen (only) were authorized to play radios during study hour, mine was off. A second-class midshipman had come to see me about something, long forgotten. Suddenly, the door to our room burst open, and Murray Frazee, occupant of the adjoining room and a close friend, yelled: "Turn on the radio! The Martians have landed in New Jersey!" Bizarre though this sounded, we could hear other nearby radios coming on at high volume, and we listened transfixed. Suddenly the second classman spoke: "My class ought to have permission to hear this!"

Here, at least, was a concrete idea; the duty officer in the main office could give such permission, and in any case, he should be informed. Already in my pajamas, I grabbed my bathrobe and took off. My room was on the top deck of the Second Battalion, and the main office was some distance away. Several midshipmen, also listening to the broadcast, were standing in the doors of their rooms as I ran by.

I burst into the duty officer's quarters adjoining the main office. Lieutenant (junior grade) C. C. Kirkpatrick, years later a Superintendent of the Naval Academy, was behind the desk, obviously surprised at my unceremonious entry.

"What's up, Beach?" he barked.

"Turn on the radio!" I said urgently. As Kirkpatrick did so, the luridly dramatic depiction was in full gear, and his face turned ashen. We heard the crushing noises of the monsters going about their grisly business and the radio announcer's desperate calls for help. Then came the welcome news that aircraft were coming in from Langley Field—and suddenly, out came Kirkpatrick's Pencil and paper and he began jotting down some figures. "That's too fast," I heard him say. Then he began to twirl the tuning knob and as he did so his face gradually returned to normal. Although the New Jersey station continued to broadcast the vivid details of combat as our aircraft arrived on the scene, no other radio station, near Langley Field or elsewhere, made mention of the emergency.

Finally, with a decisive flip of his wrist, Kirkpatrick turned off the radio. "Go back to your room, Beach," he said, "we've been had."

My slow progress back to the fourth deck of the Second Battalion has three memories, all crystal clear. The first was the voice of my classmate Jack Munson, on watch as Midshipman in Charge of the main office. "Is this *The Washington Post*?" he said to the telephone. "No, we've heard nothing about it. Midshipmen are not allowed to have their radios on during study hour. What did you say is happening?"

Bless you Jack, I thought, as I went on my way. My second memory is that nearly all the doors to all the rooms in the hallways where I passed were open, and a number of wisecracks came at me as I went by. On my own floor, however, near my room, all the doors were shut—and this is my third memory.

The story, of course, could not be contained. Everyone in Bancroft Hall was titillated, secretly delighted of course at not having himself become involved. Our weekly *Midshipman's Log* magazine carried a cartoon showing me racing down the halls, bathrobe streaming behind like the tail on a comet, and to this day the story occasionally comes up, normally considerably improved.

But there was a word of comfort, too, later dropped my way by a wartime skipper: "Too bad you could not have traded places with the young Army guy who didn't report the radar contact when the Japanese attacked Pearl Harbor."

Retired Captain Beach is the best-selling author of *Run Silent, Run Deep*, *Keepers of the Sea*, *The U.S. Navy: A 200-Year History*, *Scapegoats*, and several other books and articles of fiction and nonfiction, all associated in some form with naval and seafaring history. A decorated veteran of World War II, he is the first submarine skipper to circumnavigate the earth submerged and was naval aide to President Dwight D. Eisenhower.

Jimmy Carter, Class of 1947

My most memorable experience was our youngster cruise on the USS *New York* (BB-34). My cleaning assignment was near the huge steam engine pistons, in the after head. Everything throbbed together. Sanitary fixtures were a trough on each side of the compartment, flushed by a stream of salt water.

There was a torpedo scare on the return leg of our cruise, and the ship zigzagged violently. Suddenly, there was a crunching sound, and one of our four propellers was bent severely. For those working in the stern, it was a moot question whether the ship collided with a torpedo or a reef.

With every rotation of the screw, the after stern bounced a few inches—just enough to throw the flushing water and a large portion of the excrement onto the deck. Our cleaning attempts helped me to understand the Greek myth of Sisyphus, forever rolling his stone uphill in Hades.

The regular crew had bunks, but many of us midshipmen had to sleep on deck, using our kapok lifejackets as combination mattresses and pillows. We were required to wear them when not sleeping. A symbolic event occurred as the ship entered her destination harbor, when one of our lifejackets fell overboard, and promptly sank.

> **Mr. Carter** was the 39th President of the United States. Since his presidency, he has written eight books and has been active in national and international human rights organizations. He is also founder, with Emory University, of the Carter Center, addressing worldwide public-policy issues.

John H. Dalton, Class of 1964

The most memorable experience for me was leading the company that was formed to march in President John F. Kennedy's funeral procession. I had marched in his inaugural parade, as a plebe, with the entire Brigade of Midshipmen. At the time of President Kennedy's assassination I was in my first-class year and serving as the Deputy Brigade Commander. A special honor company was formed consisting of second- and first-class midshipmen. The Army-Navy game was scheduled for Saturday, 30 November, but it was postponed a week when President Kennedy was shot. This special company, which had not marched together before, began practicing for the parade. I had served in staff positions as a midshipman, and had never led a company unit before. Marching in that parade was an unforgettable experience. I will never forget the somber drumbeat as we marched through the streets of Washington, and noticing the thousands of people crowded on the streets to pay final tribute to President Kennedy. He was the first President in our history who had served on active duty in the Navy. Since then, five of our next seven Presidents have been former naval officers.

The most inspirational occurrence for me as a midshipman was Rear Admiral Charles C. Kirkpatrick, our Superintendent, continually reminding us at pep rallies and other meetings of the Brigade that "You can do anything you set your mind to do and don't you forget it." He was greatly admired by the Brigade of Midshipmen, and we made him an honorary member of the Class of 1964.

> A former nuclear submariner, **Mr. Dalton** is the current Secretary of the Navy.

John S. McCain III, Class of 1958

My most memorable experiences at the Naval Academy are two—one when I was making the transition from midshipman to commissioned officer, and one that took place many years afterward. The first happened at my graduation, when President Dwight D. Eisenhower delivered the address. This was a rare opportunity that I will never forget, to have seen and heard one of the greatest heroes in American history. I still remember his words to us concerning our future obligations as officers in the Armed Forces of the United States.

My other most memorable experience came when I myself spoke at the commencement proceedings of the U.S. Naval Academy. I cannot adequately describe the uplifting experience it was to shake the hands of an entire graduating class, the most wonderful group of men and women, at that given time, in the entire United States. I was honored to be in their company.

> **Senator McCain** is a Republican U.S. Senator from Arizona. He spent five-and-a-half years as a prisoner of war during the Vietnam War.

Robert C. McFarlane, Class of 1959

Just before June Week in spring 1958 I was thrilled to learn of my assignment to the carrier *Essex* (CV-38) for first-class cruise. The carrier was to operate with the Sixth Fleet in the Mediterranean. As I packed my seabag my thoughts were animated by Bancroft folklore concerning liberty on the Riviera and standing bridge watches as a junior officer. As we made the transit from Annapolis Roads to Gibraltar, however, intelligence summaries concerning rising tensions in Lebanon began to indicate that we might be in for more than receptions in whites surrounded by fair maidens. Sure enough, just after midnight on my 21st birthday, 12 July, the *Essex* was ordered out of Piraeus—leaving the entire liberty party ashore—to proceed to Lebanon in company with a Marine Amphibious Unit.

In circumstances with many parallels to what is going on in Bosnia today, rival political factions, ostensibly motivated by ethnic and religious differences, were fighting, with one of the factions being exploited by the Soviets for their own purposes. President Dwight D. Eisenhower saw the implications of the Russians' establishing a presence on the Mediterranean littoral and on the southern flank of NATO. In a matter of days, he took his message to the American people, explained how vital U.S. interests were at risk, committed publicly (and privately to the Russians) to "use all necessary means" to restore the status quo ante, ordered the Marines ashore, and loaded nuclear weapons onto the attack aircraft on board the *Essex*. I'll never forget seeing them on deck the morning we arrived off Beirut. And of course, Soviet ships cruising in the area saw them as well. The crisis was resolved within a few weeks without a shot being fired. The point was clear. A Commander-in-Chief with a depth of knowledge and experience in politico-military affairs who leads forthrightly to define the problem for Americans, defines the solution, and moves with dispatch to solve it, will be credible to friends and enemies. And because of that, we will end up saving lives.

Mr. McFarlane was President Ronald Reagan's National Security Advisor from 1983 to 1985.

Walter M. Schirra, Class of 1946

I remember a lesson taught to me by an Academy seamanship instructor, a very salty chief petty officer. "If you are ever in trouble or do not understand the drill, consult your Chief!"

I was a black-shoe ensign on board the USS *Alaska*, (CB-1) at the end of World War II, and I was amazed at how rapidly the reserves left our ship for stateside. After the dust settled, I was assigned as the number two turret officer, and a commander was the skipper of this "pocket battleship."

We were steaming toward Pearl Harbor, when I was informed that the new skipper wanted to exercise number two turret and fire a broadside while enroute. The event would go in his log book before the *Alaska* was decommissioned.

I was in trouble, and I surely did not understand the drill. Number two was higher than the other two turrets and had a compartment at the base known as the "blue room." I worked my way down to the chiefs' sanctuary and asked for help. After telling me "no problem," my chief gunner's mate gave me some personal schooling on how to be a turret officer.

We fired number two successfully and safely. I recall that early advice as a midshipman, and I shudder now, when I think of number two blowing up recently on the *Iowa* (BB-61).

Captain Schirra is the only astronaut to have flown missions in the Mercury, Gemini, and Apollo space programs. Besides his feats as an astronaut, he is well-known for his expert space commentary on CBS with Walter Cronkite and is the author of *Schirra's Space*, reissued recently by the Naval Institute Press.

12 "The Heartbeat of a Great Nation"

Jack Sweetman and revised by Thomas J. Cutler

(Selection from *The U.S. Naval Academy:
An Illustrated History*, 2nd Edition,
Naval Institute Press, 1995): 265–67

. . . ONLY ONCE in the entire history of the school had an individual returned to the academy for a second tour as superintendent; Rear Admiral Christopher R.P. Rodgers had been reappointed by President Garfield to rectify some of the problems the academy then faced. But never had the academy been headed by anyone higher than a vice admiral. Charles R. Larson, who had served as fifty-first superintendent and gone on to earn four stars, returned to the academy to become the fifty-fifth superintendent in August 1994. Larson's first tour at the academy was generally seen as a "good time" for the school. By returning in troubled times, it was hoped that Larson would be able to see what had changed, something that a neophyte superintendent would be less likely to accomplish. Larson was also an excellent choice because of his talents and reputation. The move was widely hailed as "just what the academy needs."

At the change of command, Chief of Naval Operations Admiral Jeremy M. Boorda acknowledged that there were serious challenges ahead for Larson, noting that some of the recent midshipmen "could not meet the standards of the institution" But he went on to say, "I prefer to reflect upon, to focus on, the . . . midshipmen who have succeeded." And he described these successful graduates as "officers who are more than just educated, but who truly understand what our core values are all about, who are honorable men and women, who can be counted upon to show courage in time of adversity, who have the necessary commitment to carry out the most difficult tasks and to sacrifice when necessary for the good of their shipmates, their Navy, and their Nation."

If the past has any relevance, Admiral Boorda's words ring true. After a century and a half, the United States Naval Academy had proved itself to all but the most skeptical. It had met the terms of its original charter by providing strong leadership to the navy, and it had exceeded that charter by providing strong leaders to the nation as a whole in many walks of life.

Since the days of Buchanan, Bancroft, and Chauvenet, the Naval School had become the United States Naval Academy, graduating the likes of George Dewey and Chester Nimitz, spawning innovators who measured the speed of light and harnessed the atom, and producing leaders who would achieve victory in two world wars and help to build the most powerful navy in the history of the world. The Naval Academy had produced more astronauts than any other school in the United States, including the first American in space, two of the original seven Mercury astronauts, the nation's first black astronaut, and the first female naval aviator to enter the astronaut program. Academy graduates had been elected to both houses of Congress and to the presidency. They had been captains of industry, diplomats, authors, professional athletes, judges, and doctors. They had earned Medals of Honor, Nobel Prizes, Olympic medals, and Super Bowl rings. They had served the U.S. Navy and Marine Corps as division officers, platoon leaders, navigators, diving officers, and pilots, carrying out their duties in the heat of combat, during the tense moments of cold war, and in the tedium of isolationist peace. Their remains are in Arlington National Cemetery, beneath the seven seas of the world, and in unmarked graves in distant lands.

While stone and bronze statues have preserved the memory of some Naval Academy graduates, all those who served in relative anonymity are memorialized in the strength and hopes of a great nation. And every year that strength is celebrated and those hopes revitalized when another group of aspirants raise their right hands and take the oath of office that makes them part of Naval Academy history:

I, ———, having been appointed a midshipman in the United States Navy, do solemnly swear (or affirm) that I will support and defend the Constitution of the United States against all enemies, foreign and domestic; that I will bear true faith and allegiance to the same; that I take this obligation freely, without any mental reservation or purpose of evasion; and that I will well and faithfully discharge the duties of the office on which I am about to enter: So help me God.

INDEX

40, 46; Griffin Hall, 50, 74; Halligan Hall, 78; Halsey Field House, 50; haphazard development, 33–34; Herndon Monument, 79, 128; Hubbard Boat House, 77; Isherwood Hall, 48, 50, 53, 74; land acquisitions, 32–33, 44, 46; Leahy Hall, 49; Lejeune Hall, 50; Luce Hall, 49, 72–73, 116; Macdonough Hall, 48, 68; Mahan Hall, 48, 73; Matthews Commission report, 37–41; Maury Hall, 48, 73; Max Bishop Stadium, 51; McNair Road, 75; Melville Hall, 50, 74; Mexican Monument, 82; Michelson-Chauvenet math-science complex, 50; New Naval Academy rebuilding (1899–1908), 34–41, 47–49; Nimitz Library, 50; Officers' Club, 53; officers' quarters, 36, 40, 44; Old Quarters, 47; parade ground, 33–34; Parker Road, 71; Perry Circle, 68; Phythian Road, 75; Porter Walk, 70; post–Civil War, 46–47; Preble Hall, 49; Prospect Hill, 46–47; Ramsay Road, 72; Rickover Hall, 50; Robert Crown Sailing Center, 50; Rodgers Road, 71; Sampson Hall, 48, 74; Sands Road, 77; Santee Basin, 78; Santee Road, 78; Strawberry Hill, 46; Stribling Row, 46, 47; Stribling Walk, 48, 69; Tecumseh Court, 48, 49; Thompson Stadium, 76, 130; in twentieth century, 49–50, 53–55; in twenty-first century, 51; Upshur Row, 47, 68; Uriah P. Levy Center and Jewish Chapel, 51; Wainwright Road, 79; Ward Hall, 72, 100; Worden Field, 70–71
Grundy, Acting Midshipman, 28
Guerriere, 42
Gunnery and Infantry Tactics, Department of, 21

Halligan, John, Jr., 78
Halligan Hall, 78
Halsey Field House, 50
Hamilton, James A., 92
Hamilton, John R., 81
Harriet Lane, 88
Hart, Thomas Charles, 123
Hartford, 75, 79
Hayes, W. B., 81
Hemple, Catherine, 18
Herbert, Hilary A., 41
Herndon Monument, 44, 79, 128
Hollis, Ira N., 122
Holloway, James L., III, 128–29
Houston, Thomas T., 81
Howell, R. Beecher, 123
Hubbard, John, 77
Hubbard Boat House, 77
Hull, Isaac, 72
Humphreys, Eliza, 31
Humphreys, Hector, 31
Humphreys, Joshua, 31

The Influence of Sea Power upon History (Mahan), 73, 117
The Influence of Sea Power upon the French Revolution (Mahan), 117
instruction, at sea, 3
Insurgente (French), 70, 79
Iowa, 147
Isherwood, Benjamin Franklin, 74
Isherwood Hall, 48, 50, 53, 74
Izac, Edouard Victor Michel, 123

Jamestown, 17
Japan, Perry's expedition to, 13, 27, 67, 72
Japanese Bell, 44
Java, 11, 42
Jeanette, 74
Jefferson, Thomas, 105
John Adams, 92

SERIES EDITOR

THOMAS J. CUTLER has been serving the U.S. Navy in various capacities for more than fifty years. The author of many articles and books, including several editions of *The Bluejacket's Manual* and *A Sailor's History of the U.S. Navy*, he is currently the director of professional publishing at the Naval Institute Press and Fleet Professor of Strategy and Policy with the Naval War College. He has received the William P. Clements Award for Excellence in Education as military teacher of the year at the U.S. Naval Academy, the Alfred Thayer Mahan Award for Naval Literature, the U.S. Maritime Literature Award, and the Naval Institute Press Author of the Year Award.